"I would like to be remembered as a man who never looked down on those who looked up to him . . . who stood up for his beliefs . . . who tried to unite all humankind through faith and love. And if that's too much, then I guess I'd settle for being remembered only as a great boxer who became a leader and champion of his people.

"And I wouldn't even mind if folks forgot how pretty I was."

MUHAMMAD ALI
THE GREATEST

TANYA SAVORY

TP THE TOWNSEND LIBRARY

MUHAMMAD ALI:
THE GREATEST

TP THE TOWNSEND LIBRARY

For more titles in the Townsend Library,
visit our website: www.townsendpress.com

Copyright © 2017 by Townsend Press
Printed in the United States of America

0 9 8 7 6 5 4 3 2 1

Cover photograph copyright © John Stewart

Townsend Press, Inc.
439 Kelley Drive
West Berlin, NJ 08091
cs@townsendpress.com

ISBN-13: 978-1-59194-502-4

Library of Congress Control Number:
2016957433

CONTENTS

CHAPTER 1

"**Y**ou want me to do *what?*"

Rudy Clay looked at his older brother doubtfully.

"Throw rocks at me! I'll bet you anything you can't hit me."

Rudy picked up a small stone and pulled his arm back. But he couldn't bring himself to throw it. After all, his older brother was his best friend.

"Come on!" Cassius shouted from across the front yard of their small home in Louisville, Kentucky. "I'm too fast. Watch!" He began dancing around, darting and dodging in order to prove to Rudy that he was too swift on his feet to be hit. He bobbed his head back and forth until Rudy began laughing.

"Okay, watch out!"

Rudy began tossing rocks slowly at Cassius. But when his brother easily dodged every one, Rudy started throwing faster and faster. Finally, he began hurling two rocks at a time. Not a single rock even grazed Cassius.

"Man, Cash, you *are* too fast," Rudy finally said, shaking his head.

"That's right!" Cassius shouted gleefully as he ran around the yard with his hands over his head in a victory dance. "I'm the best!"

Even at twelve years old, the boy who would one day be known to the entire world as Muhammad Ali was full of confidence, strength, and excess energy.

"He could talk so fast, just like lightning. And he never sat still," Cassius's mother, Odessa, recalled. "I was holding him one time when he was six months old, and you know how babies stretch? He had little muscular arms and he accidentally hit me in the mouth when he stretched. It loosened my front tooth and I had to have it pulled out! So I always say his first knockout punch was in my mouth."

Cassius and Rudy had so much energy that they were known as the "wrecking crew" in their Louisville neighborhood, since things always seemed to get broken when the two boys were around. Baseballs got thrown through windows, flowerpots got knocked over, and dishes got dropped. When the boys weren't breaking things, they rode their bikes, played marbles, and organized neighborhood games of tag and football. In many ways, Cassius and his younger brother lived the typical lives of boys growing up in the 1940s and 1950s.

But in many more ways, their lives were far different from those of most American boys during that era.

In parts of the South during this time, black

people were separated from white people. Many white people believed that blacks were second-class citizens and that they were not as smart, as hardworking, or even as clean as white people. For this reason, many cities throughout the South, including Louisville, had what were known as "Jim Crow" laws. These laws ensured that white people would not have to be "bothered" by the presence of black people. Blacks had to use separate bathrooms, water fountains, and even swimming pools. They were forced to the back of buses and into stuffy, crowded balcony seats in movie theaters. Black people were often not allowed to even enter white-owned restaurants. Signs on the doors bluntly announced, "No Colored People Allowed."

One of Cassius Clay's earliest memories was of walking downtown with his mother on a very hot summer day. He was extremely thirsty and began crying. Odessa Clay looked around for a black water fountain, but she couldn't find one. Finally, in desperation, she and Cassius entered a small diner.

"I'm sorry, but I was wondering if you could please let my son have a glass of water," Mrs. Clay said politely to the white man behind the counter. She gestured toward five-year-old Cassius, who had tears streaking his face. "He's just so thirsty."

The man glared at Odessa, shook his head, and pointed toward the sign by the door.

"Get out. There's nothing I can do for you."

Young Cassius held tightly to his mother's hand and stared at the white man's hateful face. He would never forget how that moment felt. It was the moment that Cassius realized that he lived in a world of separation. A black writer who lived in Louisville around the same time wrote, "On my side of the veil everything was black: the homes, the people, the churches, the schools, the Negro park with Negro park police. . . . There were two Louisvilles and, in America, two Americas."

As Cassius grew older, he quickly learned just how separated the "two Louisvilles" were. One afternoon when he was out riding his bike with a friend, they turned down an unfamiliar street and found themselves in a white neighborhood. People turned and stared at the boys. A woman hurried out of her yard and onto the safety of her porch. Finally a man pulled up beside the boys in his car and shouted, "Niggers, go home!"

Not long after this, Cassius went to a Halloween party and noticed that a girl who was dressed as a superhero had painted her face white. When Cassius asked the girl why she had made her face white, she replied, "Because my sister told me there is no such thing as a black superhero."

"She was right," Muhammad Ali would write many years later. "When I turned on the television, everyone was always white. Superman was white. They even made Tarzan, king of the jungle in *Africa*, a white man. Nothing good was reflected in our image. Even at that early age, I could see that something was very wrong. I didn't understand it. I thought my skin was beautiful."

A simmering anger and frustration began brewing deep inside the young Cassius Clay. It bothered him that his father's talent as a painter was never taken seriously, simply because of the color of his skin. While Mr. Clay dreamed of being an artist, he was reduced to painting signs for beer, groceries, and gasoline for a living. Even worse, Cassius watched his mother leave before daylight every day to go to a house in a fancy white neighborhood where she cleaned, cooked, and took care of babies for twelve hours—for barely thirty cents an hour. There was often not enough for Cassius and his brother to eat unless their mother spent her entire day's earnings on food for a complete dinner. Rain leaked through the roof of the Clays' home, because there was no money to fix it. Clothes came from Goodwill, and even when shoes got so worn out that there were holes in them, the two boys had to wear them to school.

"My father became an expert at cutting out cardboard and putting it in the bottoms of our shoes," Ali later said in his autobiography.

The separation, the name-calling, and the lack of opportunity for his parents may have frustrated and confused Cassius Clay, but one event in particular made him furious. In a small town in Mississippi, a young boy who was the same age as Cassius went into a grocery store to buy some candy. His name was Emmett Till. Like Cassius, 14-year-old Emmett was outgoing and friendly, and he talked to everyone. According to the white woman who was working behind the counter at the store, however, Emmett didn't just speak to her—he flirted with her.

Some of the white men who lived in the small Mississippi town heard about Emmitt's "crime" and hunted him down. They beat him senseless and then drowned him in the nearby river. His body was found several days later. Heartbroken and outraged, Emmett's mother refused to let her son be buried until mourners and newspaper reporters saw the boy's bashed-in and swollen face. Two pictures of Emmett, one of him handsome and smiling and one of him in his coffin, were printed in black newspapers nationwide. Cassius stared at the pictures in horror, and then the horror turned to fury.

"I couldn't get Emmett out of my mind," Ali later wrote. Looking at Emmett's face was a grim reminder of just how limited and brutal life could be for a black person in the South. "One evening, I thought of a way to get back at white people for his death."

Cassius met a friend late at night, and the two of them sneaked down to a deserted railway station. They stared at a poster of Uncle Sam, the thin white man in striped pants and a tall hat. The poster read *I Want You for the U.S. Army*, and Uncle Sam was pointing right at Cassius with a stern expression. It made Cassius so angry that he picked up handfuls of rocks and threw them at the poster, swearing at the old white man.

Next, the two boys broke into a shoeshine shed and stole two iron shoe rests. They jammed the rests into the railroad tracks and waited for a train to come along. When the train wheels hit the rests, the wheels locked up. The locked metal wheels proceeded to tear the wooden ties of the track to shreds for nearly a quarter mile. Cassius and his friend ran off laughing, but in the morning, Cassius was still angry. He knew that throwing rocks and destroying train ties was not the way to vent anger. He knew that anger should be channeled in a more productive way. But what could he do?

Unexpectedly, the answer came to him one winter afternoon. It was an answer that would change Cassius Clay's life forever.

"My bike!" twelve-year-old Cassius shouted. "My bike is gone!"

Cassius and a friend had ridden their bikes downtown to go to the Columbia Auditorium to see the Louisville Home Show, a mostly black trade show. Vendors displayed everything from window frames to gardening tools. Many of the vendors offered free candy, popcorn, and trinkets to get people's attention. Cassius and his friend spent half the day wandering around, eating the free goodies, and looking at displays. When they finally walked out in the afternoon, Cassius's brand-new red bicycle, which he had just gotten for Christmas, was gone. It had been stolen.

"I was so upset that I went looking for the police to report it," Ali later recalled. "Someone directed me down to the gym run by a local policeman named Joe Martin, who was teaching young boys to box in his spare time."

Cassius stomped into the gym, half crying and half shouting about his bike. Joe Martin came over and put his hand on Cassius's shoulder and told him to calm down.

"If I find whoever stole my bike, I'm gonna whup him!" Cassius said angrily as he wiped his nose.

Mr. Martin looked at the scrawny twelve-year-old and smiled. "Well, you better learn how to fight before you start challenging people that you're gonna whup."

Mr. Martin pointed to a makeshift boxing ring where two boys around Cassius's age were sparring with one another. They were wearing small padded helmets and big boxing gloves. Cassius watched the boys, fascinated by their skill and the way they moved around and threw punches. But the two boys in the ring were white. Cassius looked at Joe Martin, a white policeman, doubtfully.

"You'd show *me* how to fight?" Cassius asked.

"Yes sir," Martin said as he slapped Cassius on the back. "As long as you work hard and stay out of trouble, you're welcome here."

At just a little over 100 pounds, Cassius Clay

was uncoordinated and unfocused when he first began boxing. In fight after fight, he got beaten. In one fight with an older opponent, Cassius was daydreaming about a scooter he wished he could buy when a left hook hit him right in the face. It was the first of only two times Cassius would ever be knocked out in the ring. When he came to, he looked around in a daze and asked, "Where's the scooter that hit me?"

But in spite of his unimpressive beginnings, there was something people noticed about this skinny kid with the friendly grin.

"When Cassius first came in, he looked like a young colt," one young boxer remembered. "He was spindly-legged and wiry. But even then, there was an aura about him. People would stop and look and not know what they were looking at, but they were looking at *him*."

Cassius didn't have much of a punch at first, but he was fast and light on his feet. And he was completely determined to become a boxer—a great boxer. He shared his dreams with Rudy, who began tagging along with his big brother to Martin's gym. Rudy was as fascinated and excited by boxing as his brother was, and within the year, Rudy also began training. Although he would never achieve the success of his big brother, Rudy would follow in Cassius's footsteps and also become a professional boxer. From the very first moment Rudy slipped his hands into boxing gloves, Cassius encouraged his brother and talked about his own big plans.

"At twelve, he predicted he'd be the heavyweight champion of the world," Rudy later said of Cassius. "I'd say, 'Yes, and I'm going to be there with you.' We were always so close."

Cassius's positive attitude drew the attention of a black trainer, Fred Stoner, who owned a real boxing gym downtown. Soon, Cassius was training at both Martin's and Stoner's gyms. Stoner knew something about the lack of opportunity and dead ends that young black boys and men faced. He'd seen too many black kids give up and turn to the streets, drinking, and crime. Stoner saw something different in Cassius. He saw something of himself.

"Clay was a hungry fighter," Stoner recalled. "He didn't come out of a rich family. He didn't have it too easy. We fighters are all out of the same bag."

Within a few years, Cassius was training six days a week. He would go to school from eight in the morning until two in the afternoon. He worked a part-time job until six, grabbed a bite to eat, and then trained at Martin's gym until eight. From there, he headed over to Stoner's gym to learn the finer points and tricks and moves of boxing until midnight. This schedule left little time for schoolwork, but Cassius didn't care. His grades had never been very good. Cassius knew he would never go to college, so what was the point of good grades?

"Boxing was my way out; my only way out," he explained. "It became my world."

Soon, Cassius began winning fights. He wasn't a hard hitter, but he could dodge punches with lightning speed. He danced around his opponent and moved around the ring until the other fighter was exhausted. Then Cassius would finish him off.

With the first taste of success, Cassius became absolutely focused on one thing: becoming the best boxer. Not a good or very good boxer—the *best*. Everything he did, he did with boxing in mind.

"At Central High School, Clay was known as the kid who drank water with garlic, who drank milk with raw eggs, who wouldn't smoke, who wouldn't drink even soda pop, who ran and shadow-boxed as often as he walked," an old classmate remembered of the fifteen-year-old.

Cassius became unstoppable in his drive and determination. He would wake up before dawn, put on his old sneakers, and slip quietly out of the house. He'd run along the railroad tracks until he'd hear a train in the distance. In his mind, the chugging of the engines was the roar of a crowd: *"Clay! Clay! Clay!"*

Cassius pictured himself in the ring in a world-championship fight. He ran faster and faster, racing the train as it approached. As it roared past him, Cassius would lift his arms in victory and shout at the top of his lungs: "I'm the heavyweight champion of the world! I'm the greatest of all time!"

CHAPTER 2

Cassius Clay loved boxing and learning how to fight, but he hated bullies. Some of the guys at the gym wanted to learn how to box specifically so that they could frighten and intimidate others. It made them feel good to push younger kids around and be the "kings" of their neighborhoods. Cassius never felt that way. In fact, Cassius always enjoyed helping younger kids out and telling them corny jokes to make them laugh. It really bothered him to see them being picked on by a bully.

In Cassius's neighborhood, the resident bully "king" was a short, muscular kid named Corky Baker. The first time Cassius saw Corky in the halls of his school, Corky was holding a kid upside down and shaking all the coins out of his pockets and laughing.

"Corky beat up everybody and terrorized the whole neighborhood, including me," Ali remembered. "Corky made money betting on how high he could lift the ends of automobiles!"

But as Cassius grew into a stronger boxer, his confidence grew in equal proportion. By the time he was sixteen, he had begun winning nearly all the fights he entered, and he wondered if he could beat Corky in the ring. Corky was street tough, and he fought dirty. Cassius knew he'd never beat him in a fistfight, but he thought he could beat him in a boxing match where there were rules and referees.

"I could whip Corky easily," Cassius said to a friend at the gym. "Just get him in here, and I'd teach him a lesson."

Word got back to Corky about what Cassius had said, and Corky laughed out loud. He thought boxing was for sissies who couldn't really fight.

"Cassius ain't got nothin' but a big mouth," Corky said. "I'll crush him."

A date was picked for the fight, and soon half of Louisville knew about it. Cassius had begun getting a name around town as an up-and-coming fighter, but his fear of Corky had always bothered him. For several years, Cassius had avoided the bully by taking different streets to get home so he wouldn't have to confront him. He had been shoved around and threatened by the older boy many times.

"I had the feeling that unless I could whip Corky with all my training, roadwork, and boxing science, then it really wasn't much use going into boxing as a profession," Ali remembered. The fight with Corky was that important. Years later, Ali recalled that he was just as nervous heading into that fight as he was heading into any professional heavyweight championship fight.

In the first round of the fight, Corky came out throwing punches like a madman. But not one hit Cassius. He dodged every punch just as he had dodged the rocks years earlier. He danced around Corky, leaned out of Corky's reach, and generally made the older boy look foolish. In addition, Cassius landed punches that blackened Corky's eye and bloodied his nose and mouth.

Corky staggered back to his stool at the end of the round. The crowd was going crazy, cheering and chanting for Cassius. Not halfway through the second round, Corky tore off his gloves and threw them down.

"Hell no! This ain't fair!" he screamed. Then he ran out of the gym in tears.

All the kids from Cassius's neighborhood rushed the boxing ring.

"We're free! You're the new king of the neighborhood! You're the king!" they chanted again and again.

Cassius didn't care that much about being the "new king," but he was relieved and thrilled to have won the fight so easily. From that day on, Corky Baker never picked on anyone again. And in Cassius's mind, that victory proved he could be a boxer—a great boxer. It was time to move on to bigger and better things. He had shown Louisville what he could do. Now it was time to show the world.

***

By 1958, 16-year-old Cassius Clay had won two national Amateur Athletic Union boxing titles, six Kentucky Golden Gloves titles, and two national Golden Gloves championships. In all of his amateur fights combined, Cassius won 100 fights and lost only five. And those losses were early in his amateur career. More and more, it was beginning to look like no one could beat Cassius Clay.

In just a few short years, Cassius had developed his own unique fighting style. He was not a hard hitter, but his constant dancing, dodging, and movement in the ring confused opponents and wore them down. Furthermore, he avoided punches by leaning back. Most coaches frowned upon this technique, pointing out that it was awkward. But to Cassius, the technique felt natural, so he ignored the advice to stop. Leaning back confused his opponents even more. They weren't sure how to land a hit on someone who did that. Their trainers had never taught them how to fight a "leaner," since so few boxers intentionally used this technique.

And there was something else unusual about Cassius.

"Look at me! I'm the best! Y'all lookin' at a champion! Ain't nobody better than Cassius Clay!"

Cassius was becoming as well known for his over-the-top bragging and loud mouth as he was for his boxing skills. No one had ever seen anything like it. Most boxers didn't say much at all—they tended to keep quiet, answering fans' and reporters' questions in as few words as possible. And certainly no young black boxer had ever been so brash, even going so far as taunting his white opponents. But Cassius was never mean-spirited about it. His brags were always accompanied by a sly smile. When he won fights, Cassius was always complimentary and kind to his opponents.

Some people loved Cassius's behavior and found it funny and refreshing. Others were annoyed and angered by it, calling Cassius "The Louisville Lip" or simply "The Mouth." One irritated white sports reporter wrote, "One of these days, someone will shut Clay's mouth up with a strong left hook. That day can't come too soon. He needs to learn a lesson!"

But that day never came, and the lesson in losing remained unlearned. Cassius just kept on winning. In late 1958, Stoner and Martin told Cassius that they thought he had a shot at winning the gold medal at the 1960 Olympics in Rome, Italy. Naturally, Cassius heartily agreed with his trainers.

"But you're gonna have to put in a lot of work these next two years," Stoner said. And then he bluntly added, "And keep your damn mouth shut."

Cassius laughed and shook his head. "Keeping quiet ain't gonna be easy, but I'm not afraid of hard work," Cassius said. Then he just had to add, "Man, I'm not afraid of anything!"

It turns out, however, that Cassius was, in fact, afraid of one or two things.

"Oh no, oh no, oh *noooo*," eighteen-year-old Cassius moaned, his head in his big shaking hands. After two years of work, Cassius and Joe Martin were flying to San Francisco for the United States Olympic boxing trials. There, Cassius would have to win a series of fights against other American boxers in order to go to the Olympics. Cassius had never been on a plane before, and his first experience terrified him.

"It'll be okay," Martin assured his young boxer. But when the old airplane had to make its way through a storm cloud, lurching and swaying abruptly through air pockets and lightning, Cassius panicked.

"What if the wing snaps off?" Cassius asked between gasps and sobs.

"It won't."

"But what if it *does?*" Cassius insisted as he glanced in terror out the window. He silently vowed to never set foot on an airplane ever again.

For all his fear in the air, Cassius was as confident as ever once back on the ground. The San Francisco press had done its part to rile up spectators by portraying Cassius as a loudmouthed punk who shouldn't even be allowed in the ring with the "respectable" young fighters. Some people in the crowd booed Cassius and shouted rude things, but Cassius ignored them. One after another, he defeated his opponents. He had punched his ticket for the Olympics in Rome!

There was only one small problem . . .

"I'm not flying. I'll take a train or a boat," Cassius announced stubbornly a month before the Olympics.

"Trains don't go to Italy, and a boat takes so long, the Olympics would be over by the time you got there," Martin explained matter-of-factly. "You're flying. Case closed."

Cassius thought seriously about not going to the Olympics at all, he was so afraid.

"Then I thought about what my father always said," Ali said years later. "He said to always confront the things you fear. I realized that we are only brave when we have something to lose and we still try. We can't be brave without fear."

Cassius agreed to fly. But he still called the United States Air Force and asked how many plane crashes there had been between the United States and Rome. He was somewhat relieved when the official-sounding voice on the other end of the phone simply said, "None." Even so, Cassius bought a parachute and sat with it on his lap all the way to Rome, Italy.

"Hi! What's your name? Where are you from? I'm Cassius Clay from Louisville, Kentucky, and I'm gonna win the gold medal in boxing! You gotta come and watch me fight!"

Cassius was like a kid in a candy shop in the

Olympic Village in Rome. Athletes from every corner of the world were there, and Cassius was determined to meet every single one of them and boast about his skills in his friendly way.

"I'm telling you all here and now," Cassius shouted to a group of athletes and three reporters from *Sports Illustrated* magazine, "there ain't no if, ain't no maybe. I'm gonna win, and that's all there is to it!"

The other athletes loved it. They all knew that confidence in sports was a positive, not a negative. Also, Cassius's swagger was balanced with honest friendliness and an appealing charm that attracted everyone he met.

"If the athletes had had to vote for mayor of the Olympic Village, Cassius would have won," Cassius's roommate at the Village recalled.

In spite of his ease in making friends and talking (a lot!) about himself, there was something that scared Cassius almost as much as flying: girls. Even though he was very good-looking, athletic, outgoing, and funny, Cassius became very nervous and quiet around girls, particularly pretty girls. The very first time he kissed a girl at the end of a date, a year earlier, he had been so nervous that he actually passed out. The strongest boxers could not knock Cassius out, but a petite seventeen-year-old girl could. In Rome, Cassius gazed shyly at the female athletes, in awe of their strength and beauty. In particular, he was drawn to Wilma Rudolph, the young black track star from Tennessee. But, mostly,

Cassius just followed Wilma around, watching her bashfully from a safe distance.

"He'd sit there still as a rock if girls were looking at him," a friend from high school recalled. "And they looked at him all the time. Man, it scared him to death!"

But in the boxing ring, Cassius remained fearless. In the Olympics, boxers fight just three rounds. Generally, it is very hard to knock out an opponent in only three rounds, so the boxers are given points for how many punches they land and how many they avoid. But in spite of how very unlikely it would be to have a knockout in round one, Cassius strutted around before his matches crowing a quick rhyme: "This guy must be done / I'll stop him in one!" This was the beginning of the taunting, playful, and often funny rhymes that would become Muhammad Ali's trademark.

Nonetheless, Cassius did not manage a knockout in Rome. He did, however, stun his opponents with his quick feet and lightning-fast pace in the ring. No one had ever seen a young boxer who was as big as Cassius move that quickly.

"Clay had a skittering style," one reporter wrote, "like a pebble scaled over water."

Some critics didn't think much of that style, claiming that all Cassius did was sprint around the ring until he'd worn his opponent down. Then he'd throw a flurry of light, stinging punches at the exhausted boxer. To some, this didn't seem like "real boxing." Where were the huge hits?

Why didn't this boxer stand still and just slug his opponent like other boxers?

Regardless of naysayers, Cassius beat opponents from all over the world. In his final match against a much more experienced boxer from Poland, Cassius gave the older boxer two black eyes in the third round. The kid from Louisville with the wide smile and twinkling eyes had won the Olympic gold medal! The fight had been shown on television around the world. Many of the young athletes believed that this meant Cassius would be rich and famous.

"That gold medal is worth a million dollars," a white athlete told Cassius on the flight back to the United States. "You got it made now!"

Cassius believed it. When he returned to Louisville, crowds at the airport cheered. There was a parade through the city, and the mayor shook Cassius's hand heartily. The mayor let him know that the gold medal was Cassius's "key to the city," a phrase that suggested that Cassius would be happily welcomed anywhere he went in Louisville. Cassius believed this too. After all, he had made his hometown proud, and he expected a hero's welcome. The local paper even printed a poem Cassius had written on the flight back to the United States. (It refers to "Cassius of Old" because a famous Roman of ancient times also had that name.)

To make America the greatest is my goal,
So I beat the Russian, and I beat the Pole

And for the USA won the Medal of Gold.
Italians said, "You're greater than
        Cassius of Old."

We like your name, we like your game,
So make Rome your home, if you will.
I said I appreciate kind hospitality,
But the USA is my country still,
'Cause they're waiting to welcome
        me in Louisville.

For a week or so, Cassius felt as though all his dreams had come true. He truly believed that he would no longer have to endure unfair treatment in Louisville just because of his skin color. And he was so proud of his medal that he never took it off.

"I ate with it and wouldn't stop sleeping with it even though the sharp edges cut my back when I rolled over. Nothing would ever make me part with it," Ali later remembered.

But one morning, Cassius woke up and looked at the "gold" on his medal. It was beginning to rub off. He stared at it for a long time. He wondered why a country as rich as the United States hadn't made the medal out of real gold. The discovery that the top award was only painted metal took a bit of the magic out of it.

As the young champion got out of bed and stretched, little did he realize that by that evening, there would be no magic left at all in his treasured gold medal.

CHAPTER 3

"**N**o, man! Not there!"

Cassius and his friend Ronnie had been riding their motorbikes around Louisville when Cassius pointed to a restaurant where he wanted to stop. It was a restaurant in a white part of town—a place where blacks were not welcome.

"It's okay, Ronnie," Cassius assured his friend. "They'll know who I am." With a grin, Cassius tapped the medal around his neck.

The two young men walked in and sat down at the counter. Everyone in the restaurant stopped talking and turned to stare at Cassius and Ronnie. A nervous waitress cast a confused glance at the young men, then back at the owner who was working the grill. Finally, she walked over with her order pad.

"Two hamburgers and two vanilla shakes," Ronnie said quickly.

But the owner, an older white man in an apron, walked out of the kitchen. He shook his head at the waitress.

"We can't serve you here," the waitress said quietly. White boys at a nearby table began snickering and making rude comments. Cassius recognized the boys from a rival high school football team on the other side, the white side, of the city.

"Ma'am, I'm Cassius Clay. The Olympics champion," Cassius said with a polite smile. "See?" He pulled the medal from beneath his jacket and showed it to the waitress and then to the owner.

"I don't give a damn who you are," the owner said angrily as he pointed toward the door. "We don't serve no niggers!"

Stunned and furious, Cassius thought briefly about throwing a punch at the restaurant owner. Then he thought about giving the owner a piece of his mind. But he looked around the room at the white faces glaring at him, the football boys with their fists already clenched, and Cassius knew there was nothing he could do. *Nothing* had changed.

"Whatever illusions I had built up in Rome were gone," Ali later wrote. "My Olympics honeymoon was over."

An old black woman who worked in the kitchen was cleaning off a table, and she caught Cassius's eye. As he and Ronnie walked toward the door, the old woman grasped Cassius's arm and whispered, "Keep the faith, son. Such a nice poem you wrote for the paper."

Then she slipped a small book into the pocket of Cassius's jacket. Cassius assumed it was either a Bible or a religious tract. He just looked in her tear-filled eyes for a moment, and then he and Ronnie tore off on their motorbikes. Cassius felt the old ache rush through him. It was as bitter as the icy rain that began falling as the two boys rode back to their side of town.

"I felt a miserable pain in my head and my stomach," Ali remembered. "It was the pain that comes from punches you take without hitting back."

As the two boys rode their motorbikes over the Ohio River, Cassius stopped on the bridge and looked down at the rushing water. Suddenly, he tore the gold medal off his neck and hurled it angrily into the river far below.

"Are you crazy?" Ronnie shouted. "Why did you do that?"

Cassius just shook his head. "That thing ain't worth nothing. It can't even get me a damn hamburger."

(Although Muhammad Ali tells this story of throwing his medal in the Ohio River in his autobiography, *The Greatest*, some friends of Ali's say this never happened. They claim that the medal was later lost, but it was never thrown in the river. Either way, true or not, the story makes clear how disappointed and angry eighteen-year-old Cassius was.)

Late that night, Cassius was still awake, pacing miserably around his room, when he remembered the small book the old woman at the restaurant had slipped into his pocket. Pulling it out, he saw that it was a book of poems by a

black poet named Langston Hughes. Cassius
sat down on his bed and began reading one of
Hughes's most famous poems:

> *I, too, sing America*
> *I am the darker brother.*
> *They send me to eat in the kitchen*
> *When company comes,*
> *But I laugh,*
> *And eat well,*
> *And grow strong.*
>
> *Tomorrow,*
> *I'll be at the table*
> *When company comes.*
> *Nobody'll dare*
> *Say to me,*
> *"Eat in the kitchen,"*
> *Then.*
>
> *Besides,*
> *They'll see how beautiful I am*
> *And be ashamed—*
>
> *I, too, am America.*

Cassius thought about that poem, the
unfairness that surrounded him *in his own
country*. He thought about the desperate need
for change, and a new fire began burning in him.
Though still a few months shy of his nineteenth
birthday, Cassius had already begun seeing a clear

direction, path, and purpose for his life. And that purpose went well beyond boxing.

"The more injustice I saw, the stronger my feelings grew," Ali wrote. "It made me feel that I was here for a reason."

Cassius knew that if he wanted to make a career out of boxing, he would need to become a professional. As an amateur, he had gained recognition and earned his way to the Olympics. (Only amateur athletes were allowed to compete in the Olympics.) He could not earn money as an amateur—only professional boxers make money. But professional boxers also *need* money when they are starting out. They have to pay trainers and assistants, gym fees, equipment fees, and travel expenses.

Cassius dreamed of buying his parents a new car and getting Rudy a motorbike with money he knew he'd win on the professional boxing circuit. But he would need someone to sponsor him first. A sponsor was someone who would invest in Cassius. Typically, sponsors take a percentage of a boxer's winnings in exchange for paying for training and travel. It can be a gamble for the investor—if the boxer works hard and wins a lot of matches, the sponsor can make a lot of money. If the boxer loses, the sponsor loses his investment.

A few interested sponsors came forward as soon as Cassius returned from the Olympics, but none seemed right. One old millionaire compared Cassius to a racehorse, and though he offered Cassius a good deal, Cassius was offended by the white man's comparing him to an animal. Next, Joe Martin visited the Clay household with a contract that offered to pay Cassius only seventy-five dollars a week for *ten years.* Cassius's father was outraged.

"Nobody buys my son for seventy-five dollars!" he shouted at the white man. "The slave trade is over!"

Finally, a group of eleven rich businessmen from Louisville approached Cassius with a fair contract. Calling themselves the "Louisville Sponsoring Group," all of these men were millionaires and boxing fans. They offered to pay all of Cassius's training expenses for six years and, in exchange, they would take 50 percent of his winnings. They also offered Cassius a $10,000 advance if he signed the contract.

"That seemed like a huge amount of money," Ali later wrote. "The worn-down little house we lived in cost $4500, and my father was going to take a lifetime to pay it off."

The very first thing Cassius did with his advance was pay off the family home and buy his parents a new car. It made Cassius feel prouder than he'd ever felt—even prouder than when he'd won the Olympic medal.

The second thing Cassius did was to begin working with a professional boxing trainer. At first, the sponsors put Cassius with an older black boxer named Archie Moore. Moore trained boxers at his camp in California. For three months, Cassius tried following Moore's advice, but it just didn't feel right.

"Slow down! Stop moving so much!" Moore warned Cassius. "Just stand still and fight. And don't lean back!"

Cassius couldn't do it. He had developed a unique style that worked for him. He wasn't going to change it.

"I'm crazy about him. Everyone's crazy about him," Moore said in a phone conversation with the Louisville Sponsoring Group. "But he just won't do what I tell him to do. I think you're gonna need to bring him home."

Cassius was back in in Louisville only briefly before leaving for Miami, Florida, to work with a well-respected trainer, Angelo Dundee. Dundee had worked with some of the best boxers in the country, he had a good reputation—and he had met and been impressed with Cassius several years earlier.

In 1957, when Cassius was an up-and-coming amateur winning Golden Gloves championships, he went to see a big heavyweight fight at the Louisville fairgrounds. He was so awed by the big boxer and the boxer's energetic trainer, Angelo Dundee, that he went to Dundee's hotel and called him from the front desk.

"So I get a call from the lobby of the Sheraton Hotel. This kid says, 'Hi, my name is Cassius Marcellus Clay. I'm the Golden Gloves champion from Louisville. I won the Gloves in

Chicago. And I'm going to win the Olympics,'"
Dundee recalled. "There was nothing on TV, so
I told the kid to come on up. Three and a half
hours later, he left."

Dundee had never forgotten Cassius and
his outsize confidence and determination. And
Cassius hadn't forgotten the patient, interested
trainer who let him talk on and on about himself
and his dreams without interrupting, giving
unwanted advice, or telling him he'd never
become a champion. The two of them were a
natural fit.

"Training him was a whole different ballgame
from most fighters," Dundee later said. "You
didn't have to push. It was like jet propulsion.
Just touch him, and he took off! The important
thing was, *always* make him feel like he was the
guy. And let him fight the way he wanted to
fight, not the way *you* wanted him to fight." The
pairing of the black boxer from Louisville and
the Italian-American trainer from Philadelphia
turned out to be one of sport's great success
stories. Unlike many people involved in the often
brutal world of boxing, Dundee genuinely cared
about the boxers he worked with. To the end of
his life, he referred to Muhammad Ali as "my
kid."

Cassius lived in a cheap hotel in Miami and
spent all his time training with Dundee, studying
other boxers, and working out at the Fifth
Street Gym. The gym itself was described by
one reporter as not much more than a "scruffy

loft above a liquor shop and a drugstore." Much of the equipment was battered, and the smell of dust and sweat hung heavy in the hot, un-air-conditioned room. Even so, it was the gym of champions.

"It was the meeting place for the elite of boxing," Dundee remembered. "Everyone gathered there."

And when young Cassius Clay arrived on the scene, there was even more gathering. Everyone wanted to watch this young, outspoken, and beautiful Olympic champion. Cassius ate it up, making friends with nearly everyone he met. He was so unlike the typical boxer, who often kept to himself and walked around with a mean scowl, that his reputation grew even before he had won his first professional bouts in the ring.

"You seem a lot more sociable than the usual fighter," one curious newspaper reporter said to Cassius.

"I don't pretend to be friendly like most people do when they're trying to get on top," Cassius explained. "I *am* friendly."

But that didn't mean that Cassius wasn't working nonstop to "get on top." In addition to knowing that he had to train hard, Cassius was also unusually aware of how important it was to be noticed, promoted, and even seen as a little bizarre. One of his heroes had always been a wrestler who called himself "Gorgeous George." George was a showman like no one had ever seen before in the history of sports. George grew his hair long and dyed it platinum blond. He wore outrageous wrestling outfits and had someone spread rose petals in front of him as he entered the ring. He worked the crowd expertly, crowing loudly about how he would cheat to win if he had to. (He didn't, but it got the crowd going.)

George was a good wrestler, but what really began drawing the crowds was his wild and unexpected behavior. His wrestling matches were as much entertainment as they were sporting events. In the 1950s, Gorgeous George was one of the country's biggest stars and earned more money than any other athlete in the world. Some wrestling fans hated him and others loved him, but no one could resist watching him.

Cassius went to see George wrestle in 1961, curious what he was like in person. Before the match, Gorgeous George grabbed the microphone and bellowed about his opponent, "I'll kill him! I'll tear his arm off! If this bum beats me, I'll cut my beautiful, beautiful hair off. But that's not gonna happen, because I'm the greatest wrestler in the world!"

The crowd went crazy, screaming and yelling at George. Cassius looked around and grinned. The crowd may have "hated" George, but every single seat in the arena was filled. His opponent was barely known—everyone was here to watch George. Afterwards, Cassius got the opportunity to meet George backstage.

"A lot of people will pay a lot of money to

see someone shut your mouth," he told Cassius. George had heard about this brash young boxer with the loud mouth, and he wanted to be sure to encourage him and give him good advice. "So keep on bragging, keep on sassing, and always be outrageous."

Cassius nodded and took George's words to heart.

"I saw fifteen thousand people coming to see this man get beat," Ali later wrote. "And it was his talking that did it. I said to myself, 'This is a good idea!'"

So Cassius amped up the talking and the bragging. The more he talked, the more the Fifth Street Gym filled with curious people. One afternoon, Cassius walked over to a reporter from *Life* magazine, the most popular national magazine at the time, and told him he should do a story on him. The reporter just laughed. Cassius was an interesting kid, but most people had never heard of him, and he told Cassius so. Cassius thought quickly and grabbed the reporter by the arm and dragged him over to a quiet corner.

"I never told nobody this," Cassius said in a mysterious whisper, "but me and Angelo have a secret. I'm the only heavyweight boxer on earth that trains underwater!"

"Underwater?" the reporter asked, intrigued. "What do you mean?"

"Bring your camera to the hotel pool tomorrow, and I'll show you," Cassius replied.

The next morning, Cassius proceeded to do all kinds of punching and poses underwater, explaining that it made him faster on dry land. The reporter was amazed. He took a lot of pictures. The editors at *Life* were impressed by the photos of the muscular, handsome Cassius in the pool. They'd never seen anything like it. They ran a five-page spread of pictures of the young boxer. Suddenly, everyone across the United States was intrigued by Cassius Clay.

But the entire thing was phony. Cassius had made the story up on the spot. "I later found out that he had never once thrown a training punch in a pool," the reporter said years later with a laugh. "He couldn't even swim!"

The bragging and self-promotion was one thing, but Cassius knew he would have to back up his big talk with big wins. He put in the work and the long hours at Fifth Street. Naturally, Cassius had made a whole circle of new friends, and they often demanded that Cassius go out with them and party. While his friends drank and danced until all hours in the Miami bars, Cassius sipped orange juice and snuck out early so he could be in bed by ten o'clock. Before the sun was up, he ran for miles around Miami, drank raw eggs, and then practiced boxing until he was too exhausted to throw another punch. Although Cassius loved boxing, he did not particularly love the demanding work of training.

"I hated every minute of training," Ali once said bluntly. "But I said, 'Don't quit. Suffer now and live the rest of your life as a champion.'"

So Cassius suffered through weeks and weeks of dreaded training. And the skinny kid from Louisville grew into solid muscle. His shoulders were broad and heavy, his waist was narrow and steely, and his arms were like two powerful machines.

"In 1961, he was the most perfect physical specimen I had ever seen," one reporter wrote about Cassius. "You just couldn't improve on the guy. If someone came from another planet and said, 'Give us your best specimen,' you'd give them Cassius."

Cassius agreed.

It was time to become a champion.

CHAPTER 4

"**W**hen I'm through with him, he'll need a groundhog to deliver his mail!" Cassius shouted to the grinning reporters about his opponent, Lamar Clark, in April, 1961.

After a string of fights in Miami, Cassius was back in his hometown of Louisville. In his first few pro fights, Cassius had kept his mouth shut. He had appeared unusually quiet.

"He was a nice kid," his very first professional opponent recalled. "Just a kid and real nervous."

But the nervous kid won one fight after another. Every fighter Cassius went up against was older and more experienced, but Cassius was faster and sharper. He didn't earn a lot of money in his first several fights—one fight paid barely $200—but he gained an immense amount of confidence. By his sixth pro fight, this one against Clark, Cassius was undefeated. Suddenly, the pay shot up to over $2500 for the fight.

"I'll take him down in the second round!" Cassius rhymed for the reporters. It was the first time he had predicted when a fight would end. Gorgeous George had often used the same kind of tactic, and Cassius thought it would be good for getting attention and creating excitement.

It was.

In the first round, Cassius broke Lamar's nose. Everyone was wondering, "Would Cassius's prediction come true?" One minute and 27 seconds into the second round, Cassius threw a fast right and then a left into Lamar's face and shattered nose. Lamar staggered and fell. The fight was over. The press went crazy.

"The baby with the big mouth appears to be one of the many things boxing has been looking for," one sportswriter wrote. "Clay is called The Louisville Lip, Cash the Brash, Mighty Mouth, Claptrap Clay, and Gaseous Cassius, but he's a mighty fighter."

What does it take to be a "mighty fighter"? And what actually happens in a professional boxing match?

According to the rules when Cassius was fighting (some rules have changed), a fight was limited to fifteen rounds. Each round lasted three minutes, with a bell signaling the beginning and the end of a round. The fight ended when an opponent was either knocked down and could not get up after a ten-second count or knocked unconscious (KO). If a fighter could no longer continue fighting due to injuries or exhaustion, it was considered a technical knockout (TKO). Referees often had to decide technical knockouts, but sometimes a fighter would end the fight himself if he felt he couldn't go on. If a fight went for the full fifteen rounds without a KO or TKO, the winner was decided by a panel of judges.

Unlike a street fight, boxing is not a messy brawl. Along with the rules for how a match proceeds, there are numerous rules for conduct in the ring. No kicking, biting, head-butting, eye-poking, or punching below the belt is allowed. And when an opponent has fallen to the mat, the other fighter must back away. And, of course, padded leather gloves are worn both to protect the hands of the boxers and to lessen the damage of blows to the face.

So do all these rules make boxing easier or less frightening than "real fighting"? Hardly.

Many sports professionals consider boxing to be the most painful *and* the most dangerous of all sports. Consider that the main point of a boxing match is to hurt an opponent as much as possible—so much that punching him unconscious is considered the greatest success. For many boxing fans (and boxers), there is nothing more exciting than seeing a well-aimed punch in the face send an opponent to the mat, knocked out cold and unable to get up. In boxing, facial bones are repeatedly broken. In boxing, fighters want to see blood streaming from their opponent's nose and even eyes. In boxing, two men (and, now, women) are allowed by the referees to beat each other senseless.

While many sports see an occasional fatality (think car racing or skiing), it is estimated that injuries caused by boxing have killed more than 500 boxers since 1884. In fact, professional matches were reduced from 15 rounds to 12 rounds in 1982 when a Korean boxer, Kim Duk-koo, died following two strong punches to the head in the 14th round.

"Either he dies, or I die," Duk-koo had said of his opponent, Ray Mancini, just before the lightweight world championship fight began.

By the 12th round, it was not clear to the referee that Duk-koo was suffering as much as he may have been. Duk-koo refused to give up or to show how badly he was hurt.

"The fighters who get hurt are the courageous ones, the ones who will never surrender," a writer for ESPN wrote in 2007. "A boxer whose career is full of losses is rarely the one who gets hurt. Professional losers know when to bail out of a bout. Boxers who pay the ultimate price are the ones who will endure punishment and keep fighting."

By shortening the time in the ring, boxing officials hoped to have fewer boxers pay "the ultimate price." But since 1982, boxers have continued to die either in the ring or in the days following a fight. Almost as tragically, other boxers have survived but suffered brain damage from repeated blows to the head. Being "punch drunk" has left many fighters mentally challenged, with slurred speech and poor coordination.

In 1962, however, Cassius Clay didn't focus on all these statistics and dangers. He entered the ring fearlessly, confident of his skill. It was what made him a "mighty fighter." Cassius knew the damage that could be done in the ring. He had seen old fighters hanging out in the gym with their smashed noses, disfigured ears, and blank stares. But he never looked too long or wasted his energy worrying about what might happen to him.

"A young fighter doesn't like to look in the face of a scarred, punch-drunk member of the tribe. He might see his own future," Ali would later admit.

Thanks to his fast feet and unusual way of leaning back to avoid hits, Cassius managed to fight and win ten matches without getting knocked down once. But then in his eleventh pro fight, this one against Sonny Banks, a hard right in the third round sent Cassius reeling and then falling to the mat with a surprised expression. It was an important moment for Cassius. The first time a young boxer gets punched to the mat in a professional fight can be a turning point—a turn toward fear or toward bravery.

Sonny Banks danced over the dazed Cassius as the crowd cheered.

"That's right! Shut that boy's mouth up!"

"Show him, Sonny!"

But by the count of four, Cassius was up. Banks, certain that Cassius would be his 15th knockout, looked confused. Then he looked worried. Cassius's face had transformed into a ferocious scowl. Suddenly, Cassius came after

Sonny in a fury. He had predicted that he would take Banks in four rounds. Twenty-six seconds into the fourth round, Banks was bleeding and stumbling. The ref ended it with a TKO.

"Watching him get up off the floor against Sonny Banks and kill out the rest of the round, and then recover to win—that was the night I fell in love with the kid," trainer Angelo Dundee later said.

Some boxing fans began falling in love with Cassius, too, in spite of (or sometimes *because* of) his mouth. Boxing was not nearly as popular a spectator sport as it is today, but Cassius was bringing attention to it with his talk. And he was backing up all the talk with wins.

"I am beeeauuutiful! Man, just *look* at me. I am the greatest! No one can beat me!" Cassius shouted into the camera with a sly grin.

"What do you say to the folks who don't like all this bragging?" one reporter asked.

"I say it ain't bragging if you can back it up," Cassius replied, pointing a finger into the camera with a twinkle in his eye. Americans who had never watched a boxing match were suddenly curious about this unusual boxer. He was huge and powerful, yet his voice was soft and almost childlike. He could be brutal in the ring, yet his eyes were kind and warm, and his face was handsome to the point of being pretty. ("I'm so pretty, I can hardly stand to look at myself!" was one of Cassius's favorite lines.)

Still, in spite of Cassius's physical appeal and impressive string of wins, there were plenty of boxing fans who were not impressed. Many claimed that he had yet to fight a real challenger that would actually put him to the test. Angelo Dundee had carefully chosen Cassius's opponents, and he wasn't sure if Cassius was ready to go against a seriously tough fighter. Instead, Dundee decided to pick someone that would draw a lot of national attention. For Cassius's last fight of 1962, Dundee chose Cassius's first pro trainer, Archie Moore.

Moore was a legend in boxing. Out of 229 professional fights, he had lost only 26. He had knocked out 141 men. But in 1962, Moore was 48 years old—decades past what was considered a boxer's prime. Still, fans were excited to see a legend go up against The Mouth. More than 16,000 people packed the Los Angeles Sports Arena, and Cassius was promised $45,300, his biggest payday by more than $30,000.

> *Archie's been living off the fat land—*
> *I'm here to give him his pension plan.*
> *When you come into the fight, don't block*
> *   the door.*
> *'Cause you'll all go home after round four!*

Cassius followed through with his prediction. The trainer who had tried to make Cassius change his dancing and fast-moving fighting style fell to the mat in round four. Although Moore was able to get up, he couldn't go on. All that dancing, the very thing he had told Cassius not to do, had worn the old champion out.

"I'm the greatest and the double greatest, 'cause I took him out in four just like I said I would. Ain't I beautiful?" Cassius said with a wink to a pretty girl standing near his dressing room after the fight. "Come on in and tell me what *you* think of me!"

Clearly the young star who had no fear in the ring had also lost his fear of pretty girls.

"Hello, brother."

Cassius nodded at a black man selling newspapers on a Miami street corner. The newspaper was titled *Muhammad Speaks*. Cassius picked up one of the papers and looked through it. *Muhammad Speaks* was the publication of the black religious movement named the Nation of Islam. The leader of the movement was a man named Elijah Muhammad, and his ideas and teachings were expressed in the papers. Years earlier at a Golden Gloves Tournament in Chicago, Cassius had read one of these papers closely. The ideas presented in it intrigued him.

For the most part, followers of the Nation of Islam followed the Muslim religion of Islam. In many ways, the Nation of Islam believed in the same peaceful, loving ideas that more than 1.5 billion Muslims worldwide believe in today: they believed in peace and in the preciousness of human life. However, there was one major difference. Elijah Muhammad and his followers believed that the white race was evil. They believed that 6,600 years ago, all people on earth were black or brown. Then a young man named Yacub, who was both brilliant and wicked, began speaking out against God. He was punished by being exiled to a distant island. He took his revenge by creating a "devil race" of white people. In the thousands of years since white people were created, the peaceful and prosperous lives of black and brown people, Nation of Islam followers believed, had been torn apart by white people.

Now Elijah Muhammad spoke about the cruelty of whites:

"The American white people delight in mistreating us. There is no justice for us among such people, the devils in person. They hate us if we try to be good."

Muhammad spoke about the dangers of Christianity:

"You are a people who think you know all about the Bible, but there is no hope in Christianity. It is a religion organized by the enemies of the Black Nation to enslave us to the white race's rule!"

And Muhammad spoke about total separation from whites:

"Since we cannot get along with them in peace after giving them four hundred years of our sweat and blood and receiving in return the worst treatment human beings have ever experienced, we demand complete separation in a state or territory of our own."

When Cassius had first read these ideas in *Muhammad Speaks*, he had perhaps thought they were a little extreme and unusual. Still, his anger at being turned away from restaurants, being called "boy" and "nigger," and being treated like some kind of prize animal was raw and painful. His horror over the Emmett Till story was still fresh, and his frustration over examples of whites abusing blacks was increasing daily. Even in his professional fights, Cassius sensed a disgusting edge of racism from white fans, particularly when he fought a black opponent.

"They stand around and say, 'Good fight, boy: you're a good *boy*,'" Ali recalled. "They just look at fighters as brutes that come to entertain the rich white people. Beat up on each other and break each other's noses, and bleed, and show off like two little monkeys for the crowd. And half the crowd is white. We're just like two slaves in that ring. The masters get two of us big old black slaves and let us fight it out while they bet: 'My slave can whup your slave.'"

So in Miami in 1961, Cassius began talking to the man selling the papers about the ideas of the Nation of Islam.

"So, you're into the teaching?" the man asked.

"Well, I've never been in the temple," Cassius said. "But I know what you're talking about."

"Brother, you are welcome to visit the temple here in Miami. We'd be proud to have Cassius Clay."

Cassius was both pleased to be recognized and curious about what went on in the temple. He attended a meeting the very next morning.

"The first time I felt truly spiritual in my life was when I walked into the Muslim temple in Miami," Ali would remember. "It wasn't like church teaching, where I *had* to have faith that what the preacher was preaching was right. . . . And I wanted to learn more."

From that first visit, Cassius would become a regular at the Miami temple. In many ways, his visits and his growing faith kept him centered and grounded. The meetings weren't solely focused on "evil white people." The speakers at the temple also often talked about how important good health and confidence were. And they encouraged a new idea: black pride.

"You deserve nothing less than the best," one speaker shouted out to the full room. "You should have all the confidence in this world!"

"That's right, brother," Cassius said quietly.

And in late 1963, Cassius Clay gathered every ounce of confidence he had. Those who had claimed that Cassius had never fought a tough opponent would no longer be able to stick to that claim.

Clay to Fight Liston! sports headlines blared across the country. *Heavyweight World Championship Fight!*

Many boxing fans couldn't believe it. There was no way this big-mouthed kid was ready to fight a world championship match against the feared Sonny Liston. Liston would kill him! Even Angelo Dundee had doubts that his boxer was ready. He tried talking Ali out of fighting Sonny so soon, but Ali, who had already accepted the challenge, told Dundee he was ready. Years later, looking back, Ali would say, "I was crazy then. But everyone wants to believe in himself. Everybody wants to be fearless."

Cassius Clay will never win this fight, the press insisted.

"Oh yes I will," replied the fearless fighter. "Just watch me."

CHAPTER 5

"This gym ain't big enough for us both, Liston!" an irritated Cassius shouted at Sonny Liston. Liston had stopped by Fifth Street Gym a month before his fight with Cassius. Liston claimed it was just to do some training, but Cassius and everyone else knew it was to try and get under the young fighter's skin.

"You scared I'm gonna catch you in it?" Liston sneered.

"I predicted that I'm gonna finish you in eight rounds," Cassius growled. "But now you poppin' your mouth off at me, I'm gonna have to cut it to six."

Liston laughed in Cassius's face. "Somebody get this little kid a piece of candy."

"You're too old and ugly to beat me," Cassius countered, sweat streaming down his face as his anger built. He moved closer to Liston, his fists clenched.

"All right, all right," Dundee said quickly. "Settle down."

Liston just shot Cassius a disgusted look. "I'm gonna hurt you *bad*," he said in a low, threatening voice as he walked out the door.

Everyone looked at Cassius. He was angry, but there was an expression on his face that the boxers and trainers rarely, if ever, saw: nervousness. Ali would later admit that Liston made him uneasy, like no other fighter before had.

"Sonny Liston was mean," remembered a Clay/Liston fight promoter. "I mean, he had everybody scared stiff. This was a guy who went to prison for armed robbery, got out, and went right back again for beating up a cop and breaking his knees. When Sonny gave you the evil eye, you shrunk to two feet tall."

Liston had won the heavyweight title by knocking the previous champion unconscious in the very first round. Some had nicknamed Liston "The Monster" because he was so big and such a hard hitter. He rarely smiled, and he was known for intimidating other boxers by staring them down before the fight began. He was not particularly friendly, and he did not enjoy talking about himself. In many ways, Liston and Cassius were complete opposites.

In spite of being nervous, Cassius talked bigger than ever leading up to the fight:

"Liston's too ugly to be the world champ. The world's champ should be pretty like me. I'm gonna put that ugly bear on the floor, and after the fight I'm gonna build myself a pretty home and use Liston as a bearskin rug. I'm gonna pound him! Whop! Whop! *Bop! Bop!*"

Liston simply said, "My only worry is how I'll get my fist outta his big mouth once I get him in the ring."

The press loved it. And the more they loved it, the more Cassius talked. But this time around, the talk had a purpose beyond bringing attention to himself. Cassius hoped his boasting would distract and upset Liston.

"I was talking, talking," Ali recalled. "I figured Liston would get so mad that, when the fight came, he'd try to kill me and forget everything he knew about boxing."

The press doubted Liston would forget everything about boxing, but they did think he would try to kill Cassius—and possibly succeed.

"Cassius must be kidding. He's crazy to go up against that deadly fighting machine," said one sportswriter.

"The irritatingly confident Cassius will enter the ring with one handicap: he can't fight as well as he can talk," said another.

And the boxing legend Rocky Marciano just shook his head and said, "I don't think Clay's decision to fight Liston is very smart."

As the fight grew nearer, the press nearly guaranteed that Cassius would lose. Ninety-three percent of the sportswriters covering the fight predicted that Liston would win. Most felt Cassius would be knocked out early in the match. If Cassius was worried or frightened, he had to hide his feelings when it came to the press. He revealed his true feelings only to one very good friend: a young man who called himself Malcolm X.

"When I was getting ready for the fight, Malcolm was especially supportive," Ali remembered. "He talked about David and Goliath and how I could beat the monster. He called me his younger brother and helped me focus on my strengths."

Like Cassius, Malcolm X was a fighter; but he was a different kind of fighter. One of the Nation of Islam's most famous and outspoken members, Malcolm believed that black people needed to be more vocal, more angry, and more disobedient when it came to fighting for civil rights. In 1963, most black people supported Dr. Martin Luther King's examples of nonviolent protest. That summer, 250,000 people had gathered for a peaceful demonstration in Washington, D.C., in support of civil rights. The March on Washington, as it was called, drew an immense amount of attention to the problems of black Americans and the need for change.

But Malcolm X thought the entire event had been a waste of time. He pointed out all the rules and regulations that *white* people had insisted upon to make the March appear the way *they* wanted it to appear: happy and harmless. Malcolm believed the fight for civil rights required a kind of revolution, not a party.

"I was there. I observed that circus!" Malcolm wrote. "Whoever heard of angry revolutionists all harmonizing 'We Shall Overcome . . . Suum Day . . .' while tripping and swaying along arm-in-arm with the very people they were supposed to be angrily revolting against? Who ever heard of angry revolutionists swinging their bare feet together with their oppressor in lily-pad park pools, with gospels and guitars and 'I Have A Dream' speeches?"

A few weeks before the fight, Cassius flew Malcolm and his family to Miami so that he could have Malcolm nearby. Some of the people who worked with Cassius, and even some members of the temple, felt that Cassius should not be seen with Malcolm. By this point, Malcolm's face and name were well known, and many white people (and even some black people) thought he was a dangerous troublemaker. Complicating matters, Cassius, who had now been going to the temple for three years, was beginning to speak his mind.

"I'm a fighter," Cassius said in an interview when asked if he agreed with Malcolm X's and the Nation of Islam's views. "I believe in the eye-for-an-eye business. I'm no cheek-turner. You kill my dog, you better hide your cat."

In another interview, Cassius said that he agreed that black people needed to be angrier and even violent if necessary. "Go on and join something," he said to his black brothers and sisters. "Join the Black Panthers (referring to a revolutionary black organization that many white Americans found extremely threatening). Join something bad."

Who *was* this rebellious new person?

Back in Louisville, Cassius's group of wealthy sponsors were disturbed by their boxer's ties to the Nation of Islam and Malcolm X. They told Cassius that if he didn't send Malcolm back home and leave the Nation of Islam, they would cancel the fight with Liston, and Cassius would never fight again.

"They must think they own me!" Cassius said angrily to Malcolm. "I'm free to be who I want to be. What if they cancel the fight?"

"Don't worry, brother," Malcolm said. "They'll never call this fight off, because they want the money. Money is the white man's God."

Malcolm X was right; the fight was not canceled. Cassius's promised pay, win or lose, was nearly half a million dollars. The Louisville Sponsoring Group's outrage over Cassius's religion and politics was not as strong as their hunger for a share of Cassius's money.

Cassius was an extremely busy young man. He often went nonstop, from the moment he woke up until he went to bed, with his training, talking to the press, studying other boxers, promoting himself, and going to the temple.

"Man, it was like he was shot out of a rocket," one of Cassius's sparring partners from the gym recalled. "Sometimes, I'd say 'relax, relax,' but he couldn't. He just couldn't."

However, Cassius did have one pastime that soothed him and calmed him down. He loved children. Whenever he had the time, Cassius visited hospitals for children. He'd kneel in front of the children, clasp their hands, and gently say, "Hey buddy" to the boys and "Hello honey" to the girls. He'd spend hours playing Monopoly, telling corny jokes, and answering their questions about boxing. Other times, Cassius would go to poor black neighborhoods and schools to visit kids.

"They're so humble and sweet, and they don't bother nobody," Cassius said of these children. "They don't have a future, and nobody really teaches them the truth."

During a visit to a hospital two days before the Liston fight, Cassius met a ten-year-old boy who was dying of cancer. Tears came to Cassius's eyes as he looked at the child. He couldn't accept that someone so young was going to die.

"I'm gonna defeat Sonny Liston just like you're gonna defeat cancer," Cassius said quietly to the boy as he squeezed his shoulder.

The little boy just looked at Cassius with a peaceful and knowing smile.

"No," he said. "I'm going to God, and I'm going to tell God that I know you."

Cassius would never forget the little boy's

strength and calm. He resolved to take that same attitude into the ring with him in two days. However, the weigh-in the very next day was anything but calm.

"Ready to rumble! Ready to rumble! This is it, you big ugly bear!"

Both Cassius and his assistant trainer began screaming at Liston as they entered the weigh-in room. Three hundred reporters and cameramen went berserk trying to get pictures of what appeared to be a crazed Cassius Clay.

"Float like a butterfly! Sting like a bee!" Cassius bellowed over and over. He had made up this phrase the day before, and it would become his trademark over the years. Next, Cassius lunged toward the startled Liston while his crew pulled him back.

"Let's fight right NOW!" Cassius yelled as sweat poured down his face and his eyes rolled wildly. "NOW!"

Liston stared at Cassius and shook his head. "You're crazy," he said with a fleeting, worried frown.

Behind Liston's back, Cassius winked at his crew. The whole thing had been a put-on.

"Liston has been bragging that he's afraid of no man," Cassius told a friend later with a mischievous grin. "But Liston means no *sane* man. Liston's got to be afraid of a crazy man."

"Nigger, you ain't gonna win the fight today," a low voice hissed over the phone early the next morning. "If Liston don't kill you, we're gonna get you."

Cassius slammed the phone down. Since the press had printed stories about his friendship with Malcolm X and his involvement in the Nation of Islam, he'd been getting occasional hate letters and threatening calls. Leading up to the fight, though, the calls had become nearly constant.

No time for distractions, Cassius thought as he closed his eyes and took a deep breath. *Gotta focus.*

The 16,000 people in the Miami Convention Center were roaring as Cassius and Liston entered the ring on February 25, 1964. The two men glared at each from their separate corners. Then the bell rang. Within a few minutes of the first round, Liston appeared frustrated. None of his strong punches were making contact.

"I just kept running, watching his eyes," Cassius said afterward. "Liston's eyes tip you when he is about to throw a heavy punch. Some kind of way, they just flicker."

By the end of round one, Cassius was looking sharper than Liston.

"You got this!" Dundee said to his fighter as he toweled him off and rubbed his shoulders. "You can beat this old bear."

To the astonishment of the press, Cassius continued to out-fight the world champ in rounds two and three. Liston threw punch after punch, wearing himself out as Cassius danced away, leaned back, and avoided damage. In round four, Cassius landed a series of stinging right crosses on Liston's face.

"I opened a cut under his left eye," Cassius explained later. "I could see he was shocked, confused, bewildered. He's never been cut in his entire career, and now his blood is spilling into the ring."

Everything was going just as Cassius and his trainer had planned until the end of round four. As Cassius sat in his corner drinking water and catching his breath, he began shouting and shaking his head.

"I can't see! I can't see!"

A terrible stinging filled both of Cassius's eyes, and tears streamed out. Dundee tried splashing water into Cassius's eyes, but nothing seemed to help. The seconds were ticking down until the bell would signal the start of the fifth round. Had Cassius been sabotaged? There had been plenty of talk about how someone might "do something" to shut up The Mouth. Cassius immediately thought that the towels or the water in his corner had been tampered with.

"Cut off my gloves! Show the world there's wrongdoing going on!"

Dundee pleaded and reasoned with Cassius. "You're winning! This is the big one. You gotta get back out there!"

"I can't fight if I can't see!"

The bell rang, and Dundee pulled Cassius to his feet.

"What am I supposed to do?" Cassius asked as he blinked furiously and shook his head.

"Run!" Dundee shouted.

For the first few minutes of the round, Cassius sprang away from Liston, moving as quickly around the ring as he could. The press loved it. The kid was giving up! He couldn't fight, so he was running away. The crowd booed and jeered. But just as suddenly, Cassius's eyes cleared. And he was furious. *Bam! Bam! Bam!* One after another, jabs stung Liston's face. By the sixth round, Liston's eyes had changed. Cassius saw a glimmer of fear in them.

"He was tired, and I was still strong. He was a changed man."

Cassius had predicted he would defeat Liston in eight rounds. When the bell rang for round seven to begin, Cassius came bounding and dancing into the ring, ready to go at it again.

But then something completely unexpected happened. Cassius saw something land on the mat near Liston.

"I just couldn't believe it—but there it was laying there," Cassius would later say.

Liston had spit out his mouthpiece onto the mat, a fighter's way of saying he'd had enough. He slumped back on his stool and just shook his head as blood trickled down his cheeks.

Across the nation, through the radios of a million listeners came the stunned voice of the famous sports announcer, Howard Cosell:

"Liston . . . is . . . not . . . coming . . . out! Liston . . . is . . . not . . . coming . . . out! The fight is over! Cassius Clay is the winner and the new heavyweight champion of the world!"

CHAPTER 6

"**E**at your words!" Cassius screamed as he pointed to the press crowding ringside to take pictures. He ran around the ring with his arms in the air. "Eat your words! I AM THE KING!"

Some of the reporters and writers grinned at the ecstatic new world champion. Others, however, shook their heads in disbelief. How on earth had this young fighter taken down the mighty Sonny Liston? More than a few in the press thought that the fight had been rigged—that Liston had been promised a huge sum of money to lose on purpose.

"Liston was one of the least physically damaged losing champions in the history of the heavyweight division!" one reporter later wrote. "It made no sense for him to quit."

Why *had* Liston quit? According to Liston's trainer, the boxer had hurt his shoulder in the very first round when he threw a punch that didn't land. In fact, the burning in Cassius's eyes had probably been caused by the ointment that the trainers had rubbed into Liston's sore shoulder. The ointment may have gotten on Cassius's gloves and then into his eyes when he put his gloves up to protect his face.

All Cassius knew was that the press had been wrong, and he was now the heavyweight champion.

"You all said Liston would kill me," Cassius said to the crowd of reporters and writers. "Now I want all of you to tell the whole world while all the cameras are on. Tell the world that I'm The Greatest."

The reporters were silent.

"Who's The Greatest?"

Silence.

"For the LAST TIME," Cassius shouted, "WHO IS THE GREATEST?"

The reporters shuffled their feet uncomfortably and finally answered in low voices, "You are."

"All right," Cassius said with a wide smile. "You got that on film, right?"

He then answered a number of questions about the fight. Out of the blue, a reporter irritated with Cassius asked a question Cassius didn't expect.

"Is it true that you're a card-carrying member of the Black Muslims?"

Cassius frowned. The reporter made it sound like it was a bad thing. Actually, Cassius did not consider himself a "black Muslim." He was simply a follower of the Muslim faith. It was true that Elijah Muhammad and the Nation of Islam believed in separation from white people, and at the time, Cassius accepted this idea. Wasn't separation what most white people in America wanted? Cassius had not yet made a public statement about his Muslim faith, but he decided it was time.

"Card-carrying? What does that mean? I believe in Allah and in peace. I don't try to move into white neighborhoods. I don't want to marry a white woman. I was baptized when I was twelve, but I didn't know what I was doing. I'm not a Christian anymore, but I know where I'm going and I know the truth," Cassius said calmly. He looked at the surprised reporters and added, "I don't have to be who *you* want me to be. I'm free to be what I want."

Many Americans were not sure what to make of this new side of Cassius Clay. When he was just the loudmouthed, sweet-faced boxer who entertained them, that was one thing. Hate him or love him, he was just a boxer putting on a show. Now he was becoming something else—something that felt threatening to many white Americans. Was Cassius going to become a radical hater of white people like his friend Malcolm X, who called white people "blue-eyed devils"? Other people thought that the Muslim faith was "anti-American." In spite of the fact that freedom of religion is a basic American right, some people felt Cassius was choosing a "foreign" religion that had no place in a mostly Christian United States.

Even Cassius's parents were very disappointed with him.

"Cassius should have never gone to Miami," Odessa Clay said through tears. "They let the Muslims steal my boy!"

It hurt Cassius deeply to upset his mother, who had devoted herself to her Baptist church for years. Still, Cassius stuck to what he believed.

"When I was growing up, my mother taught me all she knew about God," Cassius said when asked how he felt about denying his mother's Christian faith. "I've changed my religion and some of my beliefs since then, but her God is still God; I just call him by a different name."

And within only days of announcing his Muslim faith, Cassius would ask the world to call *him* by a different name, too.

"Cassius Clay is a slave name," Cassius announced in early March, 1964. "I didn't choose it, and I don't want it."

Like Malcolm X (whose original last name was "Little"), Cassius was descended from slaves. His great-grandfather had been owned by a Kentucky slaveholder who was also named Cassius Clay. The slaveholder Clay had changed his mind about slavery during the Civil War and actually worked with Abraham Lincoln to help put an end to slavery.

"My parents named me after him because he crusaded against slavery," Cassius explained. But that didn't matter; it was still a white man's name. Cassius often wondered what his real name, his African name, was. He would never know. Like Malcolm, Cassius decided to leave his old "slave" name behind. With his friend Malcolm at his side, Cassius told reporters he was changing his name to Cassius X. As with Malcolm X, "X" represented Cassius Clay's stolen African name.

However, two days later, Nation of Islam leader Elijah Muhammad decided to formally welcome Cassius as a member of the Nation and give him a true Muslim name. Elijah had always been somewhat distant toward Cassius, because he didn't approve of boxing. He also didn't approve of all the money that white men paid Cassius. But when Cassius beat Liston and became a world champion and world-famous, Elijah had a change of heart. Many people felt that Elijah was simply using Cassius for his own gain and fame. But Cassius didn't see it that way. He was thrilled and humbled to receive a new name directly from the honored leader of the Nation of Islam.

"This Clay name has no meaning," Elijah announced in a radio address on March 6, 1964. "Muhammad Ali is what I will give him as long as he believes in Allah and follows me."

Ali was pleased with his new name, which meant "one worthy of praise." Many Americans, however, were not at all happy with the new name. It would take nearly six years before the press would stop referring to Ali as Cassius Clay. And the press preyed on Americans' anxiety over this new Ali, portraying him in numerous articles as being dangerous and un-American.

"I *am* America," Ali responded angrily. "I am the part you won't recognize. But get used to me. Black, confident, cocky; my name, not yours; my religion, not yours; my goals, my own; get used to me."

It would have been much easier for Ali to keep his religious conversion and his new name private. Throughout history, plenty of powerful and famous people had chosen to hide who they really were in order to keep their fame (and flow of money) from being threatened. But Muhammad Ali was not that kind of man. He had courage both inside and outside of the ring. At the young age of 22, Ali was determined to be the person he needed to be, regardless of what others thought about him. It was a quality that would remain with him his entire life.

"I must see Africa and meet my brothers and sisters," Ali announced a few months after Elijah had given him his new name. Ali needed some distance from boxing, the fans, and the haters for a while, so he arranged a trip to several countries in Africa and the Middle East. These were parts of the world where most of the people were Muslim and had been for centuries. Called a "pilgrimage," this was a common trip for those who worshipped Allah. Ali hoped his pilgrimage would further open his eyes, his heart, and his soul to his new faith. He intended to submerge himself in the Muslim culture.

Malcolm X was on a separate pilgrimage at the same time. But Malcolm's eyes had been opened in a new way.

"There are tens of thousands of pilgrims, from all over the world. They are of all colors, from blue-eyed blondes to black-skinned Africans," Malcolm wrote in a letter. "But we were all displaying a spirit of unity and brotherhood that my experiences in America had led me to believe never could exist between the white and non-white."

Malcolm X had already begun to have doubts about Elijah Muhammad. He had long worried that Elijah was abusing his power. When he discovered that Elijah had used his position to have affairs with much younger women, he was deeply disappointed with the man he had formerly respected so greatly. Then Malcolm's experiences during his pilgrimage led him to reject the teachings of the Nation of Islam.

"We have caused injuries to some whites who did not deserve to be hurt," Malcolm declared. "I now wish nothing but happiness for all people."

Then, by sheer chance, Malcolm and Ali ran into each other in a hotel in Ghana, Africa.

"Brother Muhammad!" Malcolm shouted happily as he ran to greet his friend. But Ali would not even look at Malcolm. He had heard that Malcolm had left the Nation of Islam and broken all ties with Elijah Muhammad. At the time, Ali thought Malcolm was wrong. He just shook his head and walked away.

"Turning my back on Malcolm was one of the mistakes I regret most in my life," Ali would write years later. "I wish I'd been able to tell Malcolm I was sorry, that he was right about so many things."

Ali would never get that chance. Some members of the Nation of Islam were furious at Malcolm for leaving the brotherhood and for changing his mind about white people. On February 21, 1965, when Malcolm was speaking at a New York auditorium, three gunmen rushed the stage and shot him in front of his wife and children. Only one man was captured. He was a radical member of the Nation of Islam. Malcolm X had been shot 22 times in the chest.

"Malcolm was a great thinker and an even greater friend," Ali wrote with a heavy heart. "And Malcolm was the first to discover the truth, that color doesn't make a man a devil. It is the heart, soul, and mind that define a person."

"Elijah Muhammad and his radical thugs killed Malcolm X, and they rigged the Liston fight, too," an angry sportswriter insisted.

Many sports fans agreed. Even weeks after the Ali/Liston match, people were still grumbling about the fight and claiming that the whole thing had been a fake. For those who disliked Ali (and there were many), there was nothing they wanted more than to see a rematch in which Liston stomped Ali.

Ali was willing to fight Liston again and prove that he was worthy of his new title, but a change had come over him. After his trip to Africa, Ali saw things differently. And he felt differently about his life in America. In Africa, he had visited countries where black people were respected and powerful. They were in charge of governments and universities. No one treated them poorly or denied them rights just because of their skin color.

"Now me being heavyweight champion feels very small and cheap when I see how millions of my poor black brothers and sisters are having to struggle just to get human rights in America," Ali said when he returned home. "Black people there are free and proud—they don't feel like that over here."

Ali trained hard for the match, and he was just as determined to win as ever, but he was far quieter than he had been before the first fight with Liston. The day before the fight, Ali stayed at his home, showing movies of his trip to neighborhood black children and talking to them about his faith while reporters banged on his door.

"Why don't you want to talk about the fight?" they insisted.

"Forget the fight," Ali said quietly with a frown. "I am not concerned. The fight is won."

"But what's your prediction?" they insisted. "What round?"

"Liston ain't gonna last ten rounds. He's ugly and out of shape," Ali sighed. Then he shut the door in the reporters' faces and returned to the children to show them a magic trick.

When Liston and Ali entered the ring on May 25, 1965, many people agreed that Ali looked fitter and fresher than his opponent. But Liston was a decade older than Ali, so that was to be expected. And everyone expected Ali to dance around and throw quick, fast jabs. What no one expected was what happened barely two minutes into the first round.

"Liston has gone down!"

A seemingly easy jab on Liston's chin had sent him to the mat.

"Get up and fight, sucker!" Ali roared.

"One-two-three-four . . ." the referee began the count. Liston pulled himself up to his knees and then fell over again.

"Five! Six! Seven . . ."

The crowd erupted as Liston just sat hunched over in the ring. No one could believe it. The shortest heavyweight title fight in history had just taken place.

"What the hell just happened?" a radio announcer shouted into his microphone.

That same question was on everyone's mind. Suddenly the crowd began chanting: "Fake! Fake! Fake!"

To this day, the second Ali/Liston fight

remains one of the most disputed and questioned competitions in the world of sports. Fans and the press alike could not be convinced that Ali's quick jab could have been enough to knock Liston down for the count. Even Ali admitted that he had been surprised when Liston just sat there.

"I can tell you what happened," Liston later said. "I was down but not hurt. I saw Ali standing over me . . . Ali is waiting to hit me, and the ref can't control him. Ali is a nut. You can tell what a normal man is going to do, but you can't tell what he is going to do. He's a nut!"

Liston was not alone in calling Ali a "nut," and plenty of people called him far worse names. No one ever knew what Muhammad Ali was going to do next. He was unpredictable, and his behavior was often surprising and even shocking to many.

But one fact remained constant: Ali was never going to let anyone tell him who or what he could or could not be.

CHAPTER 7

"**M**an, I get like twenty-five phone calls a day from pretty girls, and I'm invited to thirty parties a week!" Ali bragged. "But I know they can't all *love* me. Love is a long story. If all the trees were filled with ink, and you had to write it, it never would run out—the many wonders and beauties of love."

Ali suddenly found himself chased and surrounded by beautiful women. Ali was not the shy boy who had fainted after his first kiss, but he was still inexperienced when it came to dating and relationships. At 22, he had spent nearly all of his time training and preparing for fights.

"Leave the kid alone!" Angelo Dundee would yell at the crowds of giggling girls that followed Ali to the gym. "He's a champion boxer, and he's gotta focus. Now get outta here!"

Ali wasn't looking for thirty dates for thirty parties a week; he was looking for love. He wanted to meet a girl who could show him all the "wonders and beauties of love" that he'd never known. And not long after returning from Africa, Ali thought he had found it. A 23-year-old cocktail waitress named Sonji Roi was the most beautiful girl Ali had ever seen. He started hanging around the bar where she worked, drinking orange juice and playing the jukebox, until he got up the nerve to ask her out. At the end of Ali's very first date with Sonji, he asked her to marry him.

"I didn't know if he was serious or not," Sonji later said. "But I said to myself, there's nothing else I'm doing with my life. I can be a good wife to this man."

Ali's friends thought the marriage was a bad idea. And Ali's brothers at the Nation of Islam warned him that he'd better not marry Sonji, a woman who had no interest in the Islamic faith. The brothers told Ali that he was wrong even to look twice at Sonji, much less marry her. But Ali stood his ground.

"Ain't gonna give her up," Ali said stubbornly. And in August of 1964, Ali and Sonji were married. Ali may have believed that "love is a long story," but the story of his first marriage was barely more than a few sentences. After just seventeen months, Ali and Sonji divorced. The Nation of Islam was putting pressure on Ali to "control" his wife, but Sonji, like her husband, was not going to change who she was.

"She wouldn't do what she was supposed to do," Ali recalled. "She wore lipstick, she went into bars, she dressed in clothes that were revealing. Sonji finally left me. It had to end."

Reporters joked that the only thing shorter than Ali's second fight with Liston was his marriage to Sonji. Ali didn't think the joke was funny, claiming later that he "just about went crazy" when Sonji left.

"We were all used to seeing him up and joking and laughing all the time," a friend commented after the divorce. "No one knew what to say when Cassius had a broken heart."

As the 1960s progressed, more and more Americans, both black and white, were supporting the civil rights movement. Dr. Martin Luther King's message of peace and of brotherhood between the races was becoming increasingly popular. Meanwhile, organizations like the Black Panthers and the Nation of Islam were losing popularity. White critics thought the organizations were racist. Black critics felt that the anger and violence that were often associated with these organizations only made life harder for blacks.

In spite of this, Ali continued to be outspoken when it came to remaining separate from white people. In one interview with a national magazine, Ali even stated that if a black man married a white woman, he should be killed.

"But what if a black woman marries a white man?" the interviewer asked.

"Same for her," Ali answered matter-of-factly.

When the interviewer suggested that things would be better if black and white people could live together peacefully, Ali disagreed.

"America don't have no future," he said. "America's going to be destroyed. If it doesn't do justice to the black man and separate, it's gonna burn."

Those who had known Ali before he had joined the Nation of Islam found it hard to understand how the friendly, outgoing boy had turned into such a radical and angry young man. Ali's father, who was furious when his son changed his name, believed that Elijah Muhammad had brainwashed his son. Black boxing legends Joe Louis and Floyd Patterson, both of whom Ali had always admired, tried to change Ali's mind about white people. Neither had any luck.

"Clay is so young and has been misled by the wrong people," Patterson said. "He might as well have joined the Ku Klux Klan."

Joe Louis agreed. "Clay is a good enough fighter, but it's unfortunate that he's a black Muslim. A champion should represent all groups of people, not just one."

When Ali heard these comments, he turned on his heroes. He called Patterson a "white man's Negro." He described Joe Louis as an old shuffling Uncle Tom. He claimed that both men were supporting the enemy because they owned homes in white neighborhoods.

When we think of Muhammad Ali, it is

hard to reconcile the larger-than-life legend, the smiling, friendly hero with the young man whose words and ideas seem racist in today's world. Why *did* Ali remain faithful to an organization that hurt his popularity, drove his wife away, and seemed to be connected to the murder of his best friend?

For one thing, the young Ali felt a sense of belonging and protection. He was understandably angry at the way white people had mistreated him for much of his life. It felt good to be surrounded by people who understood what he had gone through and who encouraged him to vent his anger. And the members of the Nation looked out for Ali. They provided bodyguards, managers, and even cooks for the suddenly world-famous boxer. Because of his fame and wealth, Ali worried about being taken advantage of. He believed that his brothers had his best interests in mind; this included both his brothers in the Nation and his *real* brother. Rudy Clay (who later changed his name to Rahman Ali) had long been interested in the Nation of Islam, and he actually converted to Islam before Ali did. Rahman spent as much time as possible with his big brother, often training and sparring with him. When he had told Ali a decade earlier that he'd be with him when Ali became the heavyweight champion, he had meant it. He had stood ringside at the Liston fight, screaming until he was hoarse.

And it must be remembered that Ali was quite young. He was easily caught up in the new and radical ideas that were all a part of the chaotic 1960s. In the years to come, as Ali matured and gained a better understanding of people and the world, his views on the separation of blacks and whites softened. He would no longer think of all white people as "the enemy."

"The man who views the world the same at 50 as he did at 20 has wasted 50 years of his life," Ali would famously say decades later.

And though Ali's beliefs as a young man seem racist today, many young black people admired Ali for being outspoken in a way they had never seen a black celebrity be before. Most well-known black people of that era were reluctant to speak out publicly, much less angrily, about race relations. They were afraid that it might ruin their careers. To his credit, Ali placed his ideals and his beliefs before his career. And over the next two years, Ali would be criticized and taunted for his beliefs again and again.

"I pity Clay and I hate everything he represents," a well-known writer for a New York paper wrote in 1965.

"Cassius should spend more time proving his boxing skills and less time talking," Martin Luther King, Jr. said angrily in 1966.

Ali continued boxing and winning every single fight. Some of his opponents tried rattling him by making comments about his religion or his name.

"Your Muslim faith is inferior to Christianity," black boxer Floyd Patterson said to Ali before their fight in November 1965. Ali lashed out, referring to Patterson as "white America." In response, the press jumped on Patterson's bandwagon, taking shots at Ali and making it clear that they hoped Patterson would silence Ali (or "Clay" as they insisted on calling him). When Ali destroyed Patterson in the ring, the disappointed press called Ali a cruel bully.

"His treatment of Patterson was like a little boy pulling the wings off a butterfly," the *New York Times* insisted the day after the fight. Ali had fought no differently than he ever did, but irritated white reporters began suggesting that Ali was fighting dirty and being unnecessarily brutal.

Then in February, 1967, boxer Ernie Terrell refused to call Ali by his new name.

"Why do you call me Clay?" Ali asked during a live television interview with the two boxers a few weeks before the fight. "You know my name is Muhammad Ali."

"I met you as Clay and I'm calling you Clay," Terrell said.

"It takes an Uncle Tom kind of Negro to keep calling me by my slave name," Ali said angrily.

"You've got no right to call me that," Terrell said as he leaned in threateningly toward Ali.

Ali jumped up out of his chair and took a swing at Terrell. Terrell lifted his arms to block the blow as everyone on the set pulled the two men apart. Was this just made-up drama to get viewers interested in the fight? Some believe it was. Even Terrell would later say that he thought Ali was kidding around. But come the night of the fight, Ali's anger in the ring seemed very real.

"What's my name?" he shouted at Terrell before punching him in the face.

"What's my name, Uncle Tom! What's my *NAME?*"

Terrell refused to say Ali's name, and Ali became increasingly furious. That night, he threw more punches than he had ever thrown in a fight: 737. Nearly all of them were aimed at Terrell's head. Terrell took the punishment, refusing to give up even with a broken bone beneath his eye. Finally, the fight ended with the judges' decision for Ali based on punches that had landed. Even though Ali was the clear winner, many in the crowd booed. The press called Ali a "thug" and a "torturer."

"That was a disgusting exhibition of calculated cruelty," one reporter wrote. "It was a kind of lynching."

"Cassius Clay has been the world's heavyweight champion for two years. Nobody has ever done less with his time and the title, and destroyed his image more, than Clay," a writer for the *New York Post* claimed after the fight.

It didn't matter that the entire point of a boxing match was to beat your opponent by knocking him out or by landing punches.

Suddenly Ali was the bad guy. The fact that Ali kept winning only bothered the press more. Perhaps the boxing fans who hated Ali and the press that tried to tarnish his image hoped to destroy Ali's spirit. But Ali remained as strong and defiant as ever. He continued to refuse to be controlled or changed by other people.

"We become heroes when we stand up for what we believe in," Ali said. "And it isn't always easy."

In April of 1967, Muhammad Ali would find out just how hard standing up for his beliefs could be.

For many years, the United States had been involved in a war in Vietnam, halfway around the world. The war was between North Vietnam and South Vietnam, with the communist North Vietnamese (and their fighting force, known as the Viet Cong) wanting control over the South. Because the United States opposed a communist dictatorship, we began sending advisors to South Vietnam in the early 1960s. And in 1965, we started sending American soldiers as well.

Many people in the United States were opposed to our involvement in this war, particularly young people. Young American men over the age of 18 had to register for the draft. When soldiers are "drafted," they are required to fight in a war, whether they agree with the war or not. The United States military would ultimately draft nearly 650,000 young men for the Vietnam

War. The fighting in this war was unusually difficult and dangerous. Much of the combat took place in heavy jungles full of booby traps and hidden enemy soldiers. American soldiers were often captured and tortured for months and even years by the enemy. Of the approximately 58,000 American casualties in the Vietnam War, nearly *a third* were draftees.

Young Americans took to the streets in protest, furious and heartbroken that so many of their friends, brothers, boyfriends, and husbands were being slaughtered in a war that seemed like an astounding waste of human life.

"Hell NO! We Won't Go!" became a chant that was shouted in raucous protests from coast to coast.

And true to the chant, many young men simply refused to fight. Some burned their draft cards (government-issued cards that indicated a young man might have to report for military duty) in protest and risked prison time. Others, known as "draft dodgers," fled to Canada or other countries or made up excuses for why they were unfit for military duty.

A final group avoided service by stating that they were opposed to war on moral or religious grounds. These men were known as "conscientious objectors"—their conscience, or their sense of right and wrong, would not allow them to kill other people.

It was a stormy time for the United States. For all those who protested the Vietnam War, there were at least as many Americans, at first, who supported it. Many supporters looked at the protesters with disgust. They referred to draft dodgers and conscientious objectors as cowards, criminals, and anti-American traitors.

Like every other eighteen-year-old in America, Ali had registered for the draft on his eighteenth birthday four years earlier. It was the law. But when he had taken the written test for the army, his scores had not been high enough for him to be drafted. However, as more and more men were needed for the war, the army lowered the required score.

Suddenly, in 1967, Ali's scores were good enough. Now the United States Army wanted Muhammad Ali to fight in Vietnam.

Reporters rushed madly to the cottage that Ali was renting in Miami. What would Ali say? What did he think? What will he do?

"I won't go," Ali replied firmly.

CHAPTER 8

"**W**hy should they ask me to put on a uniform and go 10,000 miles from home and drop bombs and bullets on brown people in Vietnam while Negro people in Louisville are treated like dogs and denied simple human rights?"

Ali shook his head angrily as the press continued to pound him with questions.

"So you're saying you'd be willing to go to jail?" a reporter asked excitedly. "You're refusing to go?"

"I'm not going to help murder and burn another poor nation simply to continue the domination of white slave masters of the darker people the world over. I have been warned that to take such a stand would cost me millions of dollars," Ali continued. "But I have said it once and I will say it again. The real enemy of my people is *here*. If I thought the war was going to bring freedom and equality to 22 million of my people, they wouldn't have to draft me; I'd join tomorrow. I have nothing to lose by standing up for my beliefs. So I'll go to jail, so what? We've been in jail for 400 years."

Reporters rushed back to write up the story. Ali's words made headlines around the world. In some countries, people were only mildly curious about an outspoken boxer who refused to go to war. But here in the United States, most of the media attacked Ali with a tidal wave of negativity. Members of the press who had considered him a loudmouthed troublemaker now called him a coward and worse.

"Squealing over the possibility that the military may call him up, Cassius makes himself as sorry a spectacle as those unwashed punks who picket and demonstrate against the war," a sportswriter for the *New York Herald Tribune* wrote.

"How can he expect to make millions of dollars in this country and then refuse to fight for it?" the famous black baseball pioneer Jackie Robinson demanded.

Another writer agreed with Robinson: "Clay's the worst kind of coward. He'll fight in the ring for money, but not overseas for his country."

But Ali's reasons for refusing to fight the Viet Cong had nothing to do with fear and everything to do with his faith and his conscience. Islam had taught Ali to always be at peace with those who are not his enemies. It was no secret that Ali often viewed the racist white

man in America as an enemy he would be willing
to fight. But the Vietnamese had never done
anything to Ali. No Viet Cong, he explained,
had ever called him "nigger."

"I didn't agree with the reasons why we
were in Vietnam in the first place," Ali would
later write. "More important, my religious beliefs
were not compatible with the expectations of
a soldier in combat. Islam says that all life is
sacred. I couldn't see myself trying to injure or
kill people whom I didn't even know, people
who had never done any harm to me or my
country. I didn't believe that was God's plan
for me."

Ali was ordered to report to the United
States Armed Forces Examining and Entrance
Station in Houston, Texas, on April 28, 1967.
He, along with twenty-five other young men
who had been drafted, would be formally
inducted into the Army. Outside the station, a
crowd of demonstrators gathered. They chanted
anti-war slogans and held signs that read "Draft
beer—not Ali," and "Ali—Stay Home!"

After filling out paperwork and being given
a physical exam, Ali lined up with the rest of the
men. His heart was racing, but he knew he was
about to do what he *had* to do. Ali looked at the
faces of the other men and wondered if any of
them wanted to fight in this war. How could they
kill people who had never done anything to them?

"When I call your name, you will take one
step forward," an officer suddenly announced.

"This step will indicate your induction into the Armed Forces."

One by one, the men's names were called. Each stepped forward and became a soldier. But when Ali's name was called, he stood still.

"Cassius Marcellus Clay," the officer repeated. Ali stared straight ahead, refusing to move. He felt sweat creeping down his back. *Always confront the things you fear.* His father's words echoed in his head as the officer glared. Finally, another officer approached.

"Do you understand what you are doing?" he asked quietly.

"Yes, sir," Ali replied.

"This act of refusing is a federal crime. It could result in five years in prison and a fine of ten thousand dollars."

"Yes, sir," Ali repeated. His hands shook. He had never once in his life been in trouble with the law.

"We will give you one more chance to take that step."

"I don't need it, sir."

As Ali left the station, cameras were shoved in his face and reporters closed in. Ali refused to answer their questions. An old white woman waving an American flag ran alongside Ali, laughing mockingly.

"You ain't no champ no more!" she taunted. "You ain't never gonna be a champ again! You gonna rot in jail. I hope they throw away the key!"

Ali ignored the woman's taunts, but she had been right. Almost immediately, Ali was stripped of his championship title. Within days, state by state, Ali was denied the right to compete in any kind of boxing match anywhere in the United States. His passport was taken from him so that he could not compete overseas either. For the next three years, Muhammad Ali would not be allowed to compete in the sport he had dedicated his life to. The next morning as he flew out of Houston, Ali gazed out at gathering storm clouds.

"As I flew out of Houston, I was flying into an exile that would eat up what boxing experts regard as the best years of a fighter's life," Ali recalled. But he had stood up for what was right. He had not backed down even when some of his closest friends had advised him to.

"Think of the millions of dollars you will lose!" they said. "Your fame will be destroyed!"

But Ali wasn't thinking of money or fame or even the old woman with the flag as the jet broke through the clouds and into bright sun. He thought only of how he had stayed true to his faith and his conscience.

"And I felt better than when I beat the odds and won the world heavyweight title from Liston," Ali later wrote.

Ali was not required to go straight to prison. He and his lawyers believed that his conviction was unfair, and they decided to appeal his case.

After all, Ali had stated that his reason for refusing to fight was based on his faith; he was, like so many others, a conscientious objector. For decades, Americans had been legally allowed to remain out of combat based on their religious or moral beliefs. Conscientious objection was not something new. However, it was up to the draft board to decide if an individual's commitment to his beliefs was real. And the board did not believe Ali.

"The board is not convinced that Cassius Clay is being sincere," the board declared in a formal statement.

Essentially, the board thought Ali was "making up" reasons for not wanting to fight in the war. Most members of the draft board were not familiar with the religion of Islam. They didn't understand that it was a faith based in peace, a faith that forbids its followers from killing people who are not their enemies. In particular, the draft board was suspicious of black Muslims. During the Vietnam War, hundreds of black Muslims who refused to fight were unfairly sentenced to prison. Meanwhile, plenty of white Christian conscientious objectors were legally allowed to refuse to fight. They were assigned "alternative service," such as working in schools or hospitals. It was a tremendously unfair double standard.

Ali's lawyers planned to argue Ali's case all the way up to the United States Supreme Court if necessary. But the courts were in no hurry to settle this case, and time dragged on. This is why Ali ended up in "exile," unable to fight, for over three years.

However, Ali did not waste his years in exile. He remarried, this time to a young woman named Belinda Boyd who quickly converted to Islam. Over the next several years, Ali and his second wife would have four children, including twin girls. Although Ali was often troubled and angry about the world around him, he found a release and true peace when he was with his children. He could play and tell jokes and even dress up in ridiculous costumes for hours.

"Children make you want to start life over," Ali commented, indicating that the innocence of children often made him rethink things he had said and done.

Now that he could not earn money boxing, Ali began looking for other ways to support himself and his family. He opened a chain of fast food restaurants named "Champ Burgers." Once the restaurants were up and running, Ali decided to start a speaking tour. He knew that many Americans disagreed with things he had said and done, but many others, particularly young people, saw Ali as a symbol of righteous rebellion. Here was a millionaire boxer who was willing to risk it all—money, fame, and reputation—to stand up for what was right and say *No* to the war. Suddenly, Ali was drawing huge crowds at universities and colleges across the country.

"I just put on my suit and tie, picked up my briefcase, and went out to share my beliefs," Ali later wrote. "My lectures, based on Islamic teachings, were on various subjects. They contained important insights that spoke to something deep inside me."

Ali's talks, however, were hardly formal lectures. Described as "part sermon and part rap," Ali talked about everything from the war in Vietnam to black pride to how unfair it was to be stripped of his heavyweight title. Ali spoke at more than 200 universities. Students often asked him to repeat his poetry, which he did gladly.

"My purpose was to entertain and to challenge," Ali said. His mostly white audiences were intrigued by stories of a life they couldn't imagine and by viewpoints they had never considered.

"Ali provided a window into the black world that wouldn't have been available to most of his listeners any other way," a writer for the *New York Times* explained. "Everywhere he spoke, there was excitement."

The members of Ali's audiences didn't always agree with what he said. Ali spoke out against the use of marijuana and discouraged dating between black and white students. He occasionally made sexist and anti-gay comments. But he got young people thinking about difficult topics and what many Americans considered to be radical ideas.

"I'm gonna continue fighting against the war!" Ali said at Harvard University to thunderous cheers. "Whatever the punishment for standing up for my beliefs, even if it means facing machine-gun fire, I'll face it before denouncing the religion of Islam!"

Such remarks made the United States government very nervous. Before long, the FBI issued a memo to its agents warning them about Ali.

"Clay is using his position as a nationally-known figure in the sports world to promote ideas that are completely foreign to the basic American ideals of equality and justice for all, love of God and country."

The memo went on to describe black Muslims as a dangerous "cult" that was secretly training and preparing to destroy the white race. Within a week of this outrageous memo, Ali was being followed, and all of his public appearances were closely watched by the United States Army Intelligence. After every speech, a detailed report was sent to the FBI. And then one night in 1969 . . .

"Are you Muhammad Ali?"

A motorcycle policeman had followed Ali down a dark side street in Miami. Now he leaned against Ali's car with a satisfied smile.

"There's a warrant for your arrest."

"But my case is being appealed," Ali said, confused.

"This is a warrant for a different crime," the officer replied.

Ali was stunned when he was told that he

was being taken to jail for a minor year-old traffic violation. For this "crime," Ali would sit in the Dade County jail for a week. The black prisoners far outnumbered the white prisoners.

"You wouldn't be here if you were white," more than one prisoner told Ali.

Naturally, Ali was upset about being arrested, and he noted that "jail is a terrible place," but it didn't change his mind about going to Vietnam. The FBI and Army Intelligence had, perhaps, hoped it would. After a week of prison life, some men might have had second thoughts about the possibility of spending *five years* behind bars. Ali was well aware that he might not win his case and end up in prison. But he remained strong.

"A man's got to be real serious about what he believes to say he'll do prison for five years," Ali said after he was released. "But I'm ready if I have to go."

While Ali continued to wait for his case to be decided, he earned extra money in unexpected ways. He appeared in a documentary about his refusal to go to Vietnam. He also posed for the cover of *Esquire* magazine in his boxing trunks, six arrows sticking out of his body and fake blood trickling down him. The idea the photo was attempting to express was that Ali was a martyr—a person who will suffer for something he or she believes in. Ali also acted and sang in a Broadway play and, much to everyone's surprise, he was actually very good. Even the stingiest critics praised him.

Ali also gave dozens of interviews for publications all over the world. And thanks to the help of Howard Cosell (the white Jewish sportscaster who always supported and believed in Ali), he also appeared on numerous talk shows. On one such show in late 1969, he was asked if he would return to boxing if he were allowed.

"Yeah, I'd go back if the money was right," Ali said.

Elijah Muhammad had been watching the show and was upset when he heard Ali say this. Elijah had always been against Ali boxing, because he believed it went against the peaceful message of Islam. Elijah had assumed that Ali was done with this ugly sport. He was also angry that Ali would continue to take money for what he called "entertaining white people." In the next issue of *Muhammad Speaks,* Elijah Muhammad announced, "We tell the world we're not with Muhammad Ali. Muhammad Ali is out of the circle of the brotherhood. . . ."

Elijah would eventually allow Ali back in, but this was the beginning of Ali's split with the Nation of Islam. He was starting to see things differently. During his exile from boxing, many of the friends who had stood by his side and defended him were white. Ali saw that many of these men had nothing to gain from him during this time; they simply cared about him. Skin color made no difference. Ali began questioning whether supporting the separation of blacks and whites was a good idea, after all.

And Ali wasn't the only person questioning and changing. By 1970, the majority of Americans had begun opposing the Vietnam War. Years had gone by, and many thousands of American lives had been lost. America's military support did not seem to be helping South Vietnam. Many people began thinking of the war in Vietnam as a mistake. They, like Ali, believed we should never have gotten involved in the first place.

In addition, the civil rights movement had profoundly changed the way many white Americans thought about black people. Their eyes were opened to the horrible struggles and inequality blacks had faced for generations. They began to understand why people like Malcolm X and Muhammad Ali had expressed such anger. The phrase "Black Is Beautiful" became popular. A decade earlier, an 18-year-old Cassius Clay had upset many white people when he had proudly said, "I think my black skin is beautiful! Look at me—I'm beautiful!"

But now, many people were beginning to soften their views toward Ali. Perhaps he had been a young man ahead of his time. As it turned out, he had been *right* about many things. And he had been unusually brave.

"Ali was a true warrior," Cleveland Browns football star Jim Brown said. "It was unbelievable the courage he had. He wasn't just a championship athlete. He was a champion who fought for his people. He was above sports; he was part of history."

By early 1970, Muhammad Ali had had gone from being feared and disliked to becoming a powerful symbol of both black pride and peace.

CHAPTER 9

"I strongly object to the fact that so many newspapers have given the American public and the world the impression that I have only two alternatives in taking this stand: either I go to jail or I go to the Army," Ali said in an interview about his refusal to fight in Vietnam.

"But what other alternative could there be?" the interviewer asked.

"Justice!" Ali practically shouted. "If justice prevails, if my Constitutional rights are upheld, I will be forced to go neither to the Army nor to jail. In the end, I am confident that justice will come my way, for the truth must eventually prevail."

While Ali's case slowly worked its way up to the Supreme Court of the United States, Ali was also fighting to be allowed to box again. It had not been the courts that had banned Ali from boxing; it had been the individual states' decisions. Each state had decided that Ali was "unfit" to box because he had been charged with a crime.

"But plenty of boxers have criminal records and are still allowed to fight," Ali's lawyers argued.

"There's no proof of that," athletic commissions responded.

"But just look at Sonny Liston," one lawyer pointed out.

"One example isn't enough," the commissions responded.

So Ali and his lawyers dug up *two hundred* examples of men who had been convicted of armed robbery, arson, second-degree murder, and rape, but who were still allowed to box. Ali argued that his charges were not nearly as bad. In addition, he had not even been convicted of any crime. Finally, both New York and Georgia lifted their bans.

Ali's return fight in Atlanta, Georgia, was against a fairly easy opponent, but Ali took nothing for granted. He knew the world would be watching and wondering if three years away from boxing had broken Ali's fighting spirit.

"I wasn't just fighting one man," Ali later said. "I was fighting a lot of men. I had to show them all that I was a man they couldn't intimidate. If I lost, I would have to listen to all the talk about how I had been wrong."

Ali won by a knockout in the third round. Two months later, he beat a tougher opponent with another knockout. These small, fairly easy fights were a way to ease back into boxing after so much time off, but Ali was growing impatient. He wanted his heavyweight title back. And another man had claimed it in Ali's absence: "Smokin'" Joe Frazier.

Joe Frazier was two years younger than Ali and had come of age in the amateur boxing world of Philadelphia. Philadelphia had a reputation for producing some of the most punishing boxers, and Frazier was no exception. He was an amazingly tough fighter who, like Ali, moved and bounced a great deal around the ring during a match. His punches were brutal, and he always, *always*, made crippling contact at some point. And while Ali trained hard, Frazier seemed to actually enjoy the work and trained even harder. Typically, Ali sparred with a partner for three rounds every day. Frazier sparred for eight.

Was Ali ready to fight such a tough opponent so soon?

"I was feeling like a caged tiger," Ali would explain. "I sure thought I was ready."

Many people were certain that after his long exile from boxing, there was no way Ali would ever regain the world heavyweight title; especially not from Frazier. But Ali was just as certain that these people were wrong. And though his training may not have been quite up to speed, his confidence and mouth were.

"Fifteen referees! I want fifteen referees to be at this fight because there ain't no one man who can keep up with the pace I'm gonna set except me," Ali told the press with his sly grin. "There's not a man alive who can whup me. I'm too fast. I'm too smart. I'm too pretty. You know what? I should be a postage stamp. That's the only way I'll ever get licked!"

At first, Frazier was amused by Ali's mouth. He'd known Ali for years and considered him a friend. He knew very well that before the fight Ali would brag and taunt.

"He can keep that pretty head," Frazier responded with some good-natured smack talk. "I don't want it. What I'm gonna do is try to pull his kidneys out."

But then Ali's taunts became more personal. Frazier had always been known as an athlete who steered clear of political and social issues. Ali thought this was wrong. He felt that Frazier, as a famous black athlete, should have been involved in the civil rights movement in *some* way.

"Everybody who's black wants me to keep winning," Ali said bluntly.

Frazier was irritated by this, but he kept his cool.

"He's just another Uncle Tom going along with the white man," Ali continued. "And Joe Frazier is too ugly and too dumb to be the champ. Ask Frazier, 'How do you feel, champ?' And he'll say, 'Duh duh duh' 'cause he's so stupid."

Other fighters may have found Ali annoying, but most did not really let Ali's loud mouth get to them. After all, Ali's big talk was his trademark.

Any fighter who came up against him had to expect it. But for Frazier, it was different. It really bothered him when Ali got personal. Frazier didn't care if another boxer bragged about how great he was or how he was going to win, but he believed it should end there. Opponents should show respect for one another. As Frazier felt more and more disrespected, he became angrier.

"I've got a surprise for Clay," Frazier finally said, calling Ali by his old name intentionally. "He has loudmouthed so long, he has got himself in a box. You know what I mean? The man has to do or die. I think he's going to die."

On March 8, 1971, Madison Square Garden in New York City was absolutely packed for the Ali/Frazier fight. Movie stars and other celebrities filled the best seats. The press was jammed five deep around the ring, cameras held in the air, and reporters screaming at both Ali and Frazier for final comments. Ali would earn $2.5 million dollars that night, more than four times what he had earned in any previous fight. Billed by *Sports Illustrated* magazine as "glamour versus guts," it would be the most brutal fight Ali had ever fought to date.

The two boxers slugged it out back and forth for the entire fifteen rounds. Ali was hit by Frazier more times than in all of his previous professional fights *combined*. Frazier's eyes turned black and blue and were nearly swollen shut from Ali's jabs. Then in the final round, Frazier threw a monstrous left hook that caught Ali on the jaw.

"That punch blew out all the candles on the cake!" one announcer shouted.

"Ali is down! Ali is on the floor!" another announcer screamed. "He couldn't possibly get up from a punch like that. . . . But wait . . . *Unbelievable!*"

With a dazed and pained expression, Ali stood up and fought back for two more minutes until the final bell rang. Some claimed it was the bravest performance they had ever seen from Ali. But the win went to Frazier. He had landed the most punches. Both men staggered out of the ring. Frazier's mighty punch had nearly broken Ali's jaw, and Ali's relentless battering would send Frazier to the hospital for two weeks.

To those who had supported Ali throughout his exile, this fight seemed to prove that Ali had been sincere about his beliefs. He had given up millions, and now he had finally returned to the ring and fought as hard as he could. Even those who disliked Ali had to admit that he had heart. Seeing the great Ali finally get beaten seemed to make him more likeable, more *real* to many.

"I was three and a half years out of shape," Ali said afterward. But he didn't offer that as an excuse for losing. And he readily gave Frazier the respect he deserved. "Joe punched hard. Joe earned it."

Some reporters and even fans jumped to the conclusion that Ali would never be a champion again and that his best days were over. Even Frazier thought that.

"Joe said he doesn't think you'll fight him again," one reporter said to Ali several days after the fight.

Ali just smiled and shook his head. "Oh, how wrong he is."

The Supreme Court of the United States struggled with the case of *Clay vs. United States.* Lower courts had already found Ali guilty and had agreed to the punishment of a hefty fine and prison time. Ali had to face the fact that he could have to sit behind bars for five years in payment for standing up for his beliefs.

Ali was not afraid, and he said so when asked.

"We have one life, it will soon be past," Ali famously rhymed. "What we do for God is all that will last."

If people had thought Ali was all talk and no substance, they realized now that they had been wrong. The Supreme Court was impressed. Ali's faith was real, and his reasons for not fighting in Vietnam had been honest. On June 28, 1971, the highest court in the United States accepted Ali's argument for refusing to go to war. Many other cases fought by conscientious objectors had been won, and the court realized that Ali's case was no different. Just because many Americans were unfamiliar with the religion of Islam did not make it less worthy of recognition than Christianity.

Now Ali was free to fight anywhere, anytime. For two years, Ali fought a variety of opponents in his quest to regain his fitness and, eventually, the heavyweight title. He fought some opponents more than once. One such opponent was a heavy hitter, Ken Norton. In his first fight against Norton, Ali lost when Norton broke his jaw. Ali stood in his corner wincing at the pain, shaking his head angrily, and talking nonstop.

"The jaw is broken, but The Mouth lives on," one amused reporter wrote after the fight.

Ali took some time off for his jaw to heal. During this time, he bought a large, sprawling home in New Jersey for his growing family, commenting with a laugh that he had to break his jaw in order to get any time with his kids. Ali took it upon himself to decorate the home, and visitors were often surprised by what they saw. Delicate chandeliers hung in every room, even in the bathrooms. Vases of flowers were everywhere. Exotic silk curtains rippled from ceiling to floor. Fancy gold goblets sat on the richly carved dining room table.

"I like pretty things," Ali explained to an interviewer as he reached up to gently touch the sparkling glass of a chandelier.

In 1972, Ali traveled to Saudi Arabia to visit Mecca. Mecca is considered the holiest city for the religion of Islam, and every Muslim is encouraged to visit it at least once in his or her lifetime. It was during his visit to Mecca, when he saw Muslims of every color living and worshipping in peace together, that Malcolm X had had a change of heart about white people. It would be the same for Muhammad Ali. As he walked the streets of this holy city, he realized in a very final way that he had been wrong about white people. They were not the enemy. It was true that some white people treated black people unfairly, but as in Christianity, Islam taught forgiveness and love, never hatred and revenge.

"Hating people because of their color is wrong," Ali would say after this trip. "And it doesn't matter which color does the hating. It is just plain wrong."

Ali also came to believe that his religion was not "better" than Christianity. In many ways, Christians and Muslims were actually quite similar; both believed in a God of love. Both sought peace and truth in life.

"Rivers, ponds, lakes and streams—they all are unique, but they all contain water; just as religions all contain truth," Ali observed.

Ali returned from Mecca wiser and more centered. He took this new focus and applied it to what he called the "comeback road." Though many people thought Ali could not regain the championship, Ali believed in himself. Each fight was a stepping-stone toward meeting Joe Frazier again and winning the title back. This time, Ali told himself and anyone else who would listen, he would be ready for Smokin' Joe.

And he was. Back at Madison Square Garden in January of 1974, Ali would go another twelve rounds with Frazier, but this time he would land more punches than Frazier and win. However, something unexpected had happened as Ali had traveled along his comeback road. Frazier had lost to "Big" George Foreman, a mountain of a boxer who had knocked Frazier to the mat *six times* in under five minutes, winning in only two rounds.

"Down goes Frazier!" Howard Cosell had shouted into the microphone. "And there he goes again! And again!"

Now George Foreman was the new heavyweight king. He had also recently crushed Ken Norton, the boxer who had beaten Ali and broken his jaw only ten months earlier. If ever there had been a champion who looked entirely unbeatable, George Foreman was it. Foreman, at 25, was in the peak of his boxing years, while Ali, at 32, was slowing down. The dancing, hopping, lightning-fast boxer who wore out opponents by making them chase him around the ring was gone. And Ali had never been known as a power puncher. Yet Ali set his sights on fighting Foreman next.

"It's suicide for Ali to fight Big George," one sportswriter noted. "If Ali is crazy enough to go up against Foreman, it will quite likely be Ali's last fight."

Ali read the newspapers and shook his head and smiled. He knew he wasn't in good enough shape to box Foreman yet, but he'd get there. Ali had never feared his challengers based on what the press said, and he wasn't about to start now.

"I'm not crazy, and I'm not scared," Ali said to an empty room. "Scared of *what*?"

He threw down the newspaper, went outside, and began running.

"My heart was about to break through my chest," Ali later wrote. "Sweat was pouring off me. I wanted to stop, but whenever I felt like stopping, I'd imagine George running, coming up next to me. I see him right on my heels. I push harder until slowly he fades away. . . . I've still got a long way to go, but I know I'm winning. That's right: I'm winning."

CHAPTER 10

"**A**re you out of your mind? No one anywhere in the United States is gonna pay ten million dollars for a fight!"

One of Ali's managers sat across the table from a tall man dressed in a brown tuxedo and a flashy purple bowtie. The man's name was Don King. King was a fairly inexperienced boxing promoter, but he claimed he could pull off the incredible feat of promoting the Ali–Foreman fight. Ali's manager looked at King doubtfully. Here sat a man whose hair stood straight up off his head, nearly half a foot high ("He looks like he's stuck a finger in an electric socket," was the description one writer used); a man who had been in prison yet enjoyed quoting Shakespeare; a man who had never promoted a major boxing match in his entire life. King just smiled and leaned back, puffing on a cigar.

"That's why we're going to hold the fight in Africa," King said confidently. "In the country of Zaire."

"Zai-what?" the manager asked. "Never heard of it."

"And that, my friend, is precisely why we'll be holding the fight there," King said with a broad grin.

Numerous fight promoters had wanted this fight, but King had gotten it. He had managed this unlikely feat by going separately to both Ali and Foreman and promising them five million dollars each if they would agree to fight and to let him promote it. Foreman had already turned down offers from three other promoters. Ali was certain that this was because Foreman was afraid of him.

"He wants to just hold on to the title and wait until I'm old and slow to fight me," Ali said.

But Foreman could not turn down five million dollars. He agreed, and the match was on. There was just one small problem: Don King didn't have ten million dollars, and he had no way to raise it. So King came up with a highly unusual but brilliant plan. He contacted the president of Zaire and asked if *he* would pay the boxers' fees in exchange for having the fight in his country. The president quickly said yes.

Why would the president of a rather poor country agree to this? The country of Zaire had long been ruled by Belgium. Known as the Congo for many years, the new country of Zaire had gained its independence only twelve years earlier. (In 1997, after a political revolt, the name was changed again to the Democratic Republic of the Congo.) Zaire was unknown. Most people around the world had never even heard the name *Zaire*, and its president wanted to change that. He knew that millions of people worldwide would be watching both the fight and the buildup to it. The Ali-Foreman match would basically be a two-week advertisement for Zaire. Ten million dollars was not a lot to pay for this kind of worldwide recognition.

Billed as "The Rumble in the Jungle," this fight would go down in history as, in the opinion of many, the greatest sporting event of all time. But it was much more than just a championship boxing match. Don King wanted to build anticipation and television interest, so a huge music festival was planned to coincide with the fight. B.B. King, James Brown, and a dozen other famous black musical acts boarded flights to Africa along with Ali, Foreman, and both their crews.

"It was crazy! It was beautiful and amazing," one of the concert organizers recalled. "Here were all these rich, famous, powerful black people going to Africa, going back to their homeland to celebrate and be strong. Man, *that* was black power."

And Ali, as always, did his part to build excitement and rivalry. The day before leaving for Africa, he held a press conference and unveiled his latest poetry:

I have wrestled with an alligator,
I have tussled with a whale.
I have handcuffed lightning,
And put thunder in jail . . .
Only last week, I hospitalized a brick.
Man, I'm so mean I make medicine sick!

The press laughed, but they asked Ali if he really thought he could beat Foreman. After all, even his friend Howard Cosell had said that he didn't think Ali could beat Foreman and that Ali was not the same man he had been ten years ago.

"Yeah, well I talked to Cosell's wife," Ali said with a wink. "And she says he ain't the same man he was *two* years ago!"

"But everyone knows you're not as fast as you used to be," one reporter insisted.

"Everyone don't know nothin'!" Ali barked. "I am fast, fast, fast. Look at me. I'm back in top shape. Man, I'm so fast I can turn out the light switch and jump into bed before it gets dark. When I fight Foreman, I'm gonna be dancing all night."

Foreman remained mostly quiet. People who grew up after the Rumble in the Jungle may know George Foreman only as the smiling face behind the popular cooking grills that bear his name. It would be hard for them to imagine the Foreman of 1974. He was perceived as a cold, unfriendly man of terrifying physical power. Unlike Ali, he was not particularly comfortable with interviews and cameras and talking about himself. Both he and Ali had arrived about a month before the fight to get used to the food, weather, and the new gym that had been built for them to train in. From the first moment, Foreman got off on the wrong foot with the Zairian people. He stepped off the airplane with a German shepherd on a leash—the same kind of dog that police in the former Belgian colony had used to terrorize the African residents. Foreman did most of his training in the gym, while Ali loved to go outside and run along the dirt roads and meet the Zairian people. They, in turn, were thrilled to see Ali.

"We all knew he was a boxer, of course," a local artist said. "But we also knew about what he had sacrificed for his God and his beliefs. He may have lost his title and he may have lost millions of dollars, but that is where he gained the esteem of millions of Africans."

Everywhere Ali went, crowds followed him and chanted, "Ali, *bomaye!* Ali *bomaye!*" meaning "Ali, kill him!" Ali had quickly become the people's champion.

In return, Ali praised the African people and vowed to help them.

"I want to uplift my brothers sleeping on concrete floors," he told reporters from around the world. "I want to help these people who can't eat, who live on welfare, who have no future. I'm fighting for God and my people. I'm not fighting for fame or money. I'm not fighting for me."

The excitement in Zaire continued to build in the weeks leading up to the fight. But only eight days before the fight, disaster struck. While sparring with a training partner, Foreman fell into his sparring partner's elbow. It created a bleeding gash above one of Foreman's eyes bad enough to require stitches.

"Obviously, we'll have to wait until the cut heals completely," Foreman's manager said. "No one would enter the ring with stitches."

The wait would take five weeks. At first, there was talk of calling the whole thing off, but so much time, effort, and money had already gone into the event that it would cost more to cancel it than to simply wait.

"This is the worst disappointment of all time!" Ali fumed.

But as the weeks went on, Ali came to appreciate the extra training time and the extra time with the African people. As he jogged down the roads at dawn, crowds of children would run after him, pretending to box, trying to get Ali's attention. Ali would often stop and play-box, talking gently to his admirers. Although the children couldn't understand Ali, they gathered close, their eyes sparkling with amazement.

"Man, I am gettin' so fast!" Ali reported to the press daily. "Foreman won't be able to hit me, if he can't see me. Dance, dance dance!"

Meanwhile, Foreman worked tirelessly at practicing "cornering." This is a boxing technique that some fighters use to slow down a fast-footed opponent. Basically, they move in front of the fast opponent and cut off the ring, trapping the other boxer in a corner. Foreman and his trainers knew that the key to beating Ali was to trap him. And Foreman was confident he'd beat Ali. He was the favorite by nearly 4 to 1 odds. Although far more fans worldwide were rooting for Ali, it was generally assumed that Foreman would crush Ali.

Finally, it was the day of the fight—or, rather, the *very* early morning of the fight. The fight was scheduled for 4:00 a.m. to accommodate the time zones of viewers around the world. The two boxers walked to the center of the ring as the referee explained the rules. Then Ali leaned in close to Foreman.

"You have heard of me since you were young," Ali said quietly. "You've been following me since you were a little boy. Now, you must meet me, your master!"

Foreman looked annoyed, but he just tapped Ali's glove and went to his corner. As the two men prepared for the first round, the crowd in the outdoor stadium began chanting over and over again in increasing volume:

ALI! ALI! *BOMAYE!*

ALI! ALI! *BOMAYE!*

"I felt their good vibrations, the pulse beats," Ali would later recall.

The moment the bell rang for round one, Ali rushed out and began exchanging blows with Foreman. Foreman was surprised. Why wasn't Ali dancing like he had said so many times he would? From the corner, Angelo Dundee was screaming for Ali to dance, move, get out of the way. And yet Ali stood his ground. In round two, Foreman became more confused when Ali moved to the ropes and just stood there, letting Foreman punch his body over and over again.

"My God!" Dundee bellowed. "Get off the ropes! Get off the ropes! He'll kill you!"

The chanting crowd was near hysterics by round four as Ali continued leaning against the ropes, allowing Foreman to throw one punch after another at his body as Ali protected his face. But now Ali began looking at Foreman with a fierce smile.

"Is that all you got, George? I thought you were supposed to be a hard hitter. What's wrong, George?"

At that moment, a glimmer of fear crossed Foreman's face. What was Ali doing? This was not what he had expected from the "float like a butterfly" fighter. Furthermore, Foreman had always demolished his opponents in two or three rounds. All this punching was wearing him out.

"You can't hurt me, George! You ain't *nothin'*!"

By round eight, Dundee had nearly lost his voice screaming at Ali to get off the ropes when, all of a sudden, Ali did just that.

WHAM! WHAM! WHAM!

A flurry of hard punches astonished the exhausted Foreman. He reeled and fell to the mat as the referee began the count. Foreman slowly struggled to his feet, but the count was over. Ali had used a tactic that no one had ever seen before. This "rope-a-dope" tactic, as Ali named it, had been a gamble that no one, not even Dundee, had known Ali was going to risk. But the gamble had paid off.

"Muhammad Ali has done it!" the announcer shouted. "The great man has done it!"

The Zairian crowd exploded, rushing the ring and chanting, screaming, crying. Halfway around the world in Madison Square Garden, a mostly-black crowd of 20,000 had been watching the fight on closed-circuit television. They poured out of the Garden to cheer with another 10,000 fans who had been watching outside.

"ALI! ALI! ALI! We chanted for an hour, 30,000 black men marching up 7th Avenue, stopping traffic for thirty blocks. ALI! ALI! ALI!" a black writer in the crowd recalled. "Odds didn't mean *anything*. I knew that night I would prevail as a man. As a *black* man. Ali, my champion, lit me up that night, put a fire in my chest."

As for Ali, he finally danced around the ring. "I told you so!" he shouted. "I *told* you so!"

Much later that morning, Ali was finally alone back at his private cottage. He was exhausted, but he decided to sit out on his front porch and take in a peaceful moment of the beautiful morning. Suddenly, a group of local kids surrounded Ali, smiling and waiting expectantly. More than once, Ali had performed simple magic tricks for them. Now they hoped he might show them another trick.

"I'm not sure if they even knew about my boxing or the huge match I had just won," Ali later said. "I love children because of that kind of innocence. As much as the championship meant to me, I won't ever forget sitting up with those kids that day, doing magic tricks well into the morning."

In 1975, Ali defended his title in three fights against well-known boxers who hoped to catch the aging Ali on a bad day. But even at thirty-three, Ali remained in top shape. He had bought five acres of land out in the country, about sixty miles from Philadelphia, and transformed it into a rustic training camp. Ali had longed for a place far away from the pestering press and the admiring fans who seemed to follow him everywhere. Clearly, Ali loved attention, but he also understood the importance of focus and time spent alone. He needed this focus and solitude to remain a champion, and he found that at Deer Lake.

The "Deer Lake Training Camp" contained eighteen log buildings. These included homes, training facilities, a dining hall, and even a mosque and a horse barn. Lining the roads around the camp were huge boulders. On each boulder, Ali's father had carefully painted the names of boxing greats: Rocky Marciano, Sugar Ray Robinson, Joe Louis. Ali often jogged past these boulders and thought about the work and dedication that it takes to become a champion—and remain a champion.

Just an hour away in Philadelphia, an ex-champion had been brooding for a year and a half over his loss to Ali. Joe Frazier still thought that he could beat the two-time currently reigning champ. Maybe Ali had just been lucky. In addition, the taunts from Ali and the names Ali had called Frazier had kept an angry flame burning in Smokin' Joe.

"If we were twins in the belly of our mama," Frazier said of Ali, "I'd reach over and strangle him."

Finally, plans were made for a third fight between Ali and Frazier. Don King would again promote the fight in grand style, this time in Manila in the Philippines.

Ali, who had long referred to Frazier as a "big ugly gorilla," instantly saw the opportunity for a classic rhyme.

"It's gonna be a killa and a thrilla and a chilla, when I get that gorilla in Manila," Ali announced with a broad grin at a press conference.

The press loved it. The fight was dubbed the "Thrilla in Manila," and like the "Rumble in the Jungle," it would prove to be one of the greatest boxing matches of all time.

CHAPTER 11

"Joe Frazier should give his face to the wildlife fund!" Ali said in a press conference before heading to Manila. "He's so ugly, blind men go the other way!"

"I hate Clay-Ali-whatever-his-name-is," Frazier fired back. "It's real hatred. I want to hurt him. I don't want to knock him out. I want to take his heart out. I want to take him apart piece by piece and send him back to Jesus."

Frazier had felt real pain when Ali's insults got personal, so he decided to get personal about Ali. He thought that nothing would upset Ali more than suggesting that his politics and religion were phony.

"Clay goes around the country preaching that so-called black talk," Frazier said to reporters a few days before the fight, shaking his head and pointing at Ali. "Look at him! He ain't nothin' but a big phony."

In response, Ali pulled a toy gorilla out of his pocket and held it in the air. He'd gawk stupidly at the toy and then gawk at Frazier. Then he'd punch the toy gorilla, making all the reporters roar with laughter. This made Frazier furious. Not only had he not upset Ali, now everyone was laughing at *him*! Frazier could not wait to get into the ring with Ali and kill him.

But the drama leading up to the Thrilla in Manila involved more than just the two fighters.

"You have a very beautiful wife," the president of the Philippines, Ferdinand Marcos, said to Ali. Ali, Frazier, and four guests each had been invited to the president's palace for a welcome dinner. Ali just smiled and nodded. The problem was that the woman at his side was not his wife. Ali had been seeing Veronica Porsche for more than a year, after meeting her in Zaire. She and six other women had won a beauty contest in the United States and had been hired to promote the Rumble in the Jungle.

"Veronica was one of the most beautiful women in the world," a friend of Ali's claimed. "The first time Ali saw Veronica, he fell for her instantly."

Back in the United States, Ali's wife, Belinda, saw film of Ali and Veronica. Then she heard the press commenting on Ali's "girlfriend." Belinda packed a suitcase, left their four children with family, and flew to Manila in a rage. Once there, she stormed into Ali's hotel room and had a loud and long shouting match with him that could be heard throughout the hotel. It made headlines worldwide.

"He kept Veronica a pretty good secret, but I knew something was going on," Belinda Ali would later admit. In fact, Belinda had unhappily accepted that Ali often had affairs. During their marriage, Ali fathered two daughters with other women. Though some of Ali's friends made excuses for Ali's behavior ("Women flocked to him!" "No man could resist so much temptation!" "He was rich, young, and handsome—what did his wife expect?"), Ali regretted his unfaithful behavior as he grew older.

"I used to chase women all the time," he admitted. "It hurt my wife. It offended God. And it never really made me happy. I did wrong, and I'm sorry."

In late 1975, Ali would divorce Belinda and marry Veronica, his third wife. They would have two more girls, making Ali the father of eight children by the age of 35.

"I love each child the same," Ali once said. "I try to be a good father and would do anything for them. Anything!"

One week before the fight in Manila, people were talking as much about Veronica-Belinda as they were about Ali-Frazier. Ali was distracted and stressed. Meanwhile, Frazier was preparing and relaxing in the quiet mountains outside of Manila where the air was cooler and there was no press to follow him around. Although the odds were in Ali's favor for this fight, many began to wonder if Frazier might now gain an advantage.

"Ali's a fool," Frazier said smugly. "I've always known he's crazy."

Finally, it was time for the drama, worry, and name-calling to come to an end. On October 1, 1975, more than 20,000 people jammed the Philippines Coliseum. The heat and humidity inside the coliseum were nearly unbearable. Some estimated that it was well over 100 degrees, even with the early 10:00 a.m. start.

"It was like boiling water for atmosphere," Ali's ringside doctor said. "I don't know how the fighters did it."

From the first bell, the Thrilla in Manila was a slugfest of epic proportions. Round after round, the two aging boxers pounded each other without mercy. In round six, Frazier threw a left hook that slammed Ali's head back. Ali stumbled and then looked at Frazier with a pained smile.

"They told me Joe Frazier was washed up," he said between pants.

"They lied," Frazier replied.

Ali attempted his rope-a-dope tactic, but it didn't work with Frazier. The body punches from Frazier were crushing. Ali worried that too many blows would break his ribs.

"What keeps Ali going?" the announcer asked. "How much more can he take? How much more can either man take? They're both hurt and neither wants to quit. Frazier knows Ali is in agony. But Ali, in turn, can see the swelling in Frazier's face and head."

Some watching the fight were horrified. By round twelve, there was blood dripping from both men. Frazier's eyes were so swollen that they looked like slits. Ali's face was a mask of pain. At the end of round fourteen, Ali came back to his corner and slumped over in exhaustion.

"Cut 'em off," he wheezed, holding his gloves up to Angelo Dundee. "I can't take any more. Cut off my gloves."

But Dundee looked carefully at Ali and just shook his head.

"Frazier's spittin' blood," Dundee said as he poured cold water over Ali's head. "You've got to get back out there. Just one more round."

In the opposite corner, Frazier's trainer also took a close look at his boxer. One of Frazier's eyes was completely closed, and the other eye was closing. There was no way Frazier could fight if he couldn't see.

"Joe, it's over," his trainer said firmly, even as Frazier protested that he could go one more round. His trainer shook his head. "Your eyes are swollen shut. We have to stop the fight."

This time when Ali saw his opponent give up, he did not jump up and down in excitement. He slowly stood up to be announced the winner and then collapsed on the mat with heat exhaustion.

"It was the next thing to dying," Ali said later that evening when he was feeling better. "A couple of times I felt I was leaving my body. It was insane."

When asked about Frazier's toughness, Ali offered nothing but praise for his old rival.

"I always knew he was great," Ali commented quietly. "But he's even greater than I thought he was."

After the Thrilla in Manila, Ali would never be quite the same physically. Neither would Frazier. The fight had just taken too much out of both men. Ali thought about quitting after this fight; it had been that gruesome. He knew that every great boxer had only so many matches in him before things began to unravel. And when a fighter stayed in the game too long, things could get ugly. This was always a lingering fear with aging boxers.

But as Ali had shown so many times, he was a man of remarkable courage and determination—some might say stubbornness. Some of Ali's friends began gently suggesting that he should, in fact, retire, but Ali couldn't help wondering how much more he might have left. Also, he didn't want to be seen as the type of boxer who just "sat" on his championship and didn't take the risk of defending it.

After much debating with his conscience and his will, Ali announced that he would keep on fighting.

"My toughest opponent has always been me," Ali said.

Like many boxers who have won a championship, Ali could have waited for easy matches. But Ali wanted to prove that he deserved to be called "The Greatest." He took on tough competitors, including a third match with Ken Norton.

"Norton must fall! Norton must fall!" the crowd chanted at the fight. But round after round passed, and Norton did not fall. By the end of an exhausting fifteen rounds, the decision was up to the judges. The match had been very close, but many watching the fight thought Norton had clearly won. Norton had already begun celebrating in his corner.

"I beat you! You don't win!" Norton bellowed across the ring.

But in the very narrowest of margins, the fight went to Ali. Ken Norton was stunned. He wrapped a towel around his face so that the crowd wouldn't see him crying.

"I was very bitter," Norton later said. "But not toward Ali. I've always respected him. Very few men would give up what he gave up for his beliefs, and I admire the hell out of him."

Ali remained undefeated in his six fights in 1976 and 1977. But as fans watched, they saw that the "sting" and the "float" of Ali were slowly fading. More and more often, Ali was using the ropes rather than moving quickly around his opponents. As in his fight with Foreman, Ali allowed the other boxer to batter his body with punches, hoping to wear his opponent down. This kind of beating took courage, and it also often took the full fifteen rounds. Gone were the days of Ali predicting a knockout in an early round.

Finally in February of 1978, Ali agreed to an "easy" fight against a young fighter named Leon Spinks. Spinks was a solid boxer, but he was fairly inexperienced. Ali allowed himself to ease up before the fight. He got a bit out of shape and gained a little weight. Leading up to the fight, Ali was quiet, not really thinking that the fight needed much of a buildup. Spinks, who was missing his front teeth, might have been an easy mark for Ali's jokes, but Ali said nothing. He knew that Spinks had grown up in poverty and was still too poor to fix his teeth. To mock Spinks would be, to put it in boxing terms, hitting below the belt. In addition, Spinks had nothing but admiration for Ali.

"I grew up watching Ali fight," Spinks said somewhat shyly before the fight. "He really is the greatest. I admire him so much."

Ali's plan for the fight was simple. Spinks had never fought more than eleven rounds in his career. Ali planned to let Spinks wear himself out punching Ali on the ropes. Then Ali would knock Spinks out. But the plan failed. Spinks never let up, and he kept landing punches. At the end of fifteen rounds, the judges gave the win to Spinks. Across the country, those watching the fight on TV were astounded, and in the Las Vegas Sports Arena, tears streamed down the faces of hundreds of fans. How could The Greatest have lost to this unknown kid?

"Of all the fights I lost in boxing, losing to Spinks hurt the most," Ali said. "Because it was my own fault. I wasn't in shape, and my plan for fighting him didn't work."

As for the surprised Spinks, he modestly said of his win, "I still love Ali. He's my hero! He's still the greatest; I'm just the latest."

Naturally, everyone wanted to see a rematch. Quickly. Although some close to Ali felt that he should quit, Ali strongly disagreed.

"I *have* to fight him again," Ali explained. "What they pay me doesn't matter. I want my title back. I can't leave boxing this way, losing an embarrassing fight like that."

Seven months later at the Superdome in New Orleans, Spinks and Ali met again. This time, Ali was ready, and his plan had changed. He stayed off the ropes and threw as many punches as he could. Again, the fight went the full fifteen rounds, but this time Ali won the decision. He had won the heavyweight title *three times*! No other boxer in the history of the sport had ever done that.

"I've done what I needed to do," Ali announced after the fight. "And now I'm retiring."

For two years, Ali kept himself busy making appearances on talk shows, acting in a television miniseries, and raising money in India for various charities for the poor. He was even asked by President Jimmy Carter to act as a diplomat to Africa in 1979. The United States was planning to boycott the 1980 Olympics in Russia for political reasons. Carter felt that Ali would be the perfect person to explain those reasons to the people in various African countries and ask them to join the boycott.

But not long after Ali returned from Africa, he called a friend.

"Wouldn't it be something," he said, "if I could make one more comeback?"

"Don't even think about it," the friend said.

In fact, everyone told Ali that coming back after two years off, and at his age, was a bad idea, a dangerous idea. But Ali couldn't get the idea out of his head.

"I don't know if he came back because so many people told him not to, because of the money, or if it was simply because boxing was in his blood," another friend commented. "But he came back."

The decision to return may have been bold, but it was also unwise. Ali was badly overweight at 255 pounds, and he was more out of shape than he had ever been. He returned in October of 1980 to fight Larry Holmes and it was so ugly that Dundee stopped the fight in the 11th round. Ali had lost his title for the last time.

"Oh God, that was painful to watch," said Sylvester Stallone, star of the "Rocky" movies. "It was like watching your child playing on the railroad tracks with a train coming, and you can't get him out of the way."

Ali fought and lost one final time in 1981, just one month shy of his 40th birthday.

"I'm finished," Ali finally admitted. "Father Time has caught up with me."

But there was something else aside from just age that was slowing Ali down. Ali's trainers noticed it. Thousands of fans watching the final fight on TV noticed it. There was an odd tremor in the Champ's hands and a slur in his speech now and then. Sometimes Ali appeared confused by his own slow reflexes.

At forty years old, Muhammad Ali was about to fight the most difficult fight of his life.

CHAPTER 12

"**I**'m not in any pain," Ali explained to reporters. "But I go to bed and sleep ten hours; two hours after I get up, I'm tired again. I have trembling in my hands. My speech is slurred. *I'm* not scared, but my family and friends are scared to death."

Nearly three years after Ali had fought his last boxing match, doctors were still not sure what was wrong with him. He had been tested and checked out thoroughly by all sorts of specialists, but everyone seemed to have a different idea about what might be happening.

"He's just been hit in the head too many times," one doctor pronounced. "It's not uncommon for a boxer to have mental problems like Ali's in his later years."

However, as Ali and others pointed out, Ali had *not* been hit hard in the head that often. In fact, for a retired professional boxer, Ali was remarkably unscarred and free of facial injuries. His unusual boxing style of bobbing, weaving, and leaning back had served him well.

"My face is still pretty," Ali concluded, rejecting the idea that his problems were due to too many head punches.

Another doctor tested Ali's blood and found an unusually high level of a type of pesticide in it. The doctor's theory was that for years Ali had either breathed in air or consumed water that was contaminated. Some wondered if the lake near Ali's training camp was polluted from underground dumps or nearby industries. The doctor recommended multiple "cleanings" of Ali's blood.

"The process will take many years under my close care," the doctor announced.

Some of Ali's friends and family thought that these doctors were simply trying to take advantage of Ali. At this point, Ali was worth many millions of dollars, and some doctors would have been happy to have Ali as their "project" for years. Ali refused to believe any of the more bizarre theories and continued seeking out the opinions of doctors he trusted.

Finally, in late 1984, Ali was accurately diagnosed with Parkinson's disease. People with this disease have trouble moving and speaking because of a problem with nerve cells in the brain. The brain and certain muscles no longer seem to connect. Symptoms grow more severe as those with the disease grow older. Often, the muscles in the face become rigid and stiff.

In time, victims can no longer speak or smile. Worst of all, there is no cure for Parkinson's disease.

When the news broke that Ali had Parkinson's, there was an outpouring of sympathy for him all over the world. But Ali didn't want people to feel sorry for him; and he refused to feel sorry for himself. He saw his illness as part of God's plan for him. Although Ali had once hoped to travel the world educating people about the religion of Islam after he retired from fighting, he now saw a different kind of path and opportunity. For as long as he was able, Ali would travel and make public appearances, unafraid of people seeing his trembling hands and hearing his weak voice. By doing this, he hoped that other sufferers of Parkinson's might feel braver and less ashamed.

"Knowing that others who are sick with this disease count on me gives me strength," Ali explained.

However, this didn't mean that the disease didn't often upset and frustrate Ali. At 44, he was still a fairly young man, and knowing that he had an illness that was making him old before his time was depressing and hard. After all, Ali had built a career and image based on moving quickly and speaking his mind firmly, proudly, and, quite often, loudly.

"It seems strange that I have an illness that makes it difficult for me to speak and move the way I want to," Ali said. "Those two activities once came as easily to me as breathing. Now

I have to work hard at speaking so people can understand me. I sometimes have to think about the steps I take."

Not long after being diagnosed with Parkinson's, Ali and his third wife, Veronica, divorced. This time, the decision to end the marriage was both Ali's and Veronica's. They had not been getting along well for a year or more, and they both agreed to call it quits. Even so, Ali was very sad about the divorce. He loved the family life with Veronica and their two daughters, Hana and Laila, and now with his illness, Ali worried about change—and about being alone.

"This was a sad time for Muhammad," an old friend, Yolanda Williams, said. "I've known Muhammad since I was six years old. And the first time I ever saw Muhammad cry was when he and Veronica agreed to split up."

Yolanda (or "Lonnie" as she was known) had first met Ali when she was six and he was twenty-one. Her family had moved in across the street from the Clays in Louisville, and she remembered being afraid of Cassius Clay because he was so big. But the young Cassius had been funny and friendly. He invited her, along with all the other neighborhood kids, to play Monopoly and ride bikes. He was like a big kid. Even though he was famous, he always took the time to make the neighborhood children laugh and feel important.

"Right before he fought Sonny Liston, when I was about seven, Cassius came to town in a big bus. It had a loudspeaker system, and it was painted different colors with the name 'Cassius Clay' on the side," Lonnie recalled. "He put as many kids as he could on the bus, and we drove all over town. He'd shout out, 'Who's The Greatest?' And we'd all shout back, 'You are!'"

Lonnie had never forgotten Ali's kindness and loving spirit, and she remained in touch with him through the years. When she found out he was sick, she contacted him and asked what she could do to help. He asked her to come and visit. As Lonnie comforted Ali through this difficult time, she and her old friend became closer. In 1986, Lonnie and Ali married. They would remain married for the rest of Ali's life.

"When I was 17, I knew I was going to marry Muhammad. I was just a kid in school, and I had things I needed to do, but I *knew*," Lonnie explained. One of the things Lonnie needed to do was to complete her degree in psychology from Vanderbilt University in 1978. In her thirty years of marriage to Ali, she would often note that her education and degree helped her deal with some of the more difficult aspects of Ali's failing health and how it affected both of their lives.

Muhammad Ali may have been sick, but he refused to just sit back and give up. That had never been his nature. Fighting was in his blood in more ways than one, and he intended to give life everything he could for as long as he was able.

For the next several years and into the 1990s, Ali traveled around the world with Lonnie at his side. Ali was well known worldwide, and he was welcome—even in places where other Americans were not. Ali used this advantage to do what he could to help others and to promote peace. He took medical supplies to Cuba (a country, at the time, that was off-limits to Americans) during a health crisis in that country. He flew to Sudan to bring the world's attention to the many people who were starving in that country. When Nelson Mandela, the great African peacemaker, was finally released after 27 years in prison, Ali traveled to South Africa to celebrate and shake Mandela's hand.

Perhaps most famously, Ali worked hard to free American hostages being held in Iraq. At the time, the United States and Iraq were on the brink of war. Ali met with Iraqi dictator, Saddam Hussein, and tried to persuade him that war is wrong and that all life is precious. Ali spent nearly two weeks in Baghdad. The Iraqi people swarmed him for autographs and pictures whenever he left his hotel, and Hussein thoughtfully listened to what Ali had to say.

In the end, of course, Ali was not able to persuade Hussein (or America) to avoid war, but he did gain the respect of Hussein, who released fifteen American hostages. The hostages had not even known that Ali was in Iraq, and they were surprised and overjoyed when their prison doors were suddenly flung open. Six hostages chose to fly back to the United States with Ali on a commercial jet rather than on the much-faster State Department jet.

"We did it out of sheer gratitude and respect," one hostage recalled. "I've always known that Muhammad Ali was a super sportsman, but during those hours we were together on that flight, I saw an angel."

Ali was always modest when it came to helping others, and he was sometimes genuinely uncomfortable with being thanked again and again. In his mind, his whole life had led up to this. His boxing fame was just a vehicle he could use to get *real* things done.

"All of my boxing, all my publicity was just the start of my life," Ali explained. "Now my life is *really* starting. Fighting racism, injustice, illiteracy, poverty—using this face the world knows so well and going out and fighting for truth. People still want me to say, 'I'm The Greatest! I'm this! I'm that!' But I got bigger work to do now."

As the years went by, Ali grew weaker. Sometimes he grew so tired that his voice was little more than a whisper, and his hands shook violently. Still, Muhammad Ali, like a boxer in the 15th round, refused to give up and sit down in the corner.

"The man still amazes me," George Foreman said of his old opponent. "He does the best he can every day. Ninety percent of the people who get this sick go off and hide in a corner, but not Muhammad."

And though Ali was not always comfortable with gratitude, Americans longed to show their admiration and love for such a remarkable man. From the smallest honors (Ali was the first boxer ever to appear on a *Wheaties* box) to much larger honors (he was presented the Medal of Freedom by President George W. Bush in a White House ceremony), Ali was celebrated as both a hero and a humanitarian.

In 1996, Ali received what many people think of as his most memorable honor, and certainly the most touching.

Thirty-six years after he had won gold in the Rome Olympics, Muhammad Ali stood in the shadows in the Olympic stadium in Atlanta, Georgia. Worldwide, more than three billion people were watching the opening ceremonies of the Atlanta Olympics. As always, the identity of the person who was to receive the huge honor of lighting the Olympic cauldron with the final torch had remained a secret. On the stadium track, an athlete ran with a lit torch. He lit another athlete's torch. Finally, at the base of a long ramp, the torch exchange reached the final runner, swimmer Janet Evans.

Evans jogged up the ramp, holding her burning torch high. Then she stopped at the top. A murmur of expectation rolled through the stadium as a spotlight lit the platform. Stepping slowly out of the darkness was Muhammad Ali, dressed in a white track suit. The crowd roared as Evans lit Ali's torch.

"This response he's receiving is part excitement, part affection, but especially respect," the announcer said with obvious emotion.

Ali's left arm shook badly and he walked carefully, but he held the torch high. Around the world, people cried as they watched Ali light the cauldron flame. Some cried for the champion boxer of the past. Some cried with sympathy for a sick hero. But most cried for a brave and honorable man who had come full circle. Here was the man who, as barely more than a boy, had won gold in an Olympics in a different era; an era where the honor of that gold had meant so little to a black kid from Kentucky that he had thrown his medal into the Ohio River. Here stood the man whose fierce anger, over the years, had evolved into understanding and love. Here stood the man whose loud and entertaining self-centeredness had grown into a quiet selflessness.

As the Olympic cauldron burst into flame, the old chant of "Ali! Ali!" was spoken by many in the Olympic stadium and, perhaps, by millions around the globe one final time.

With many family members by his side, Muhammad Ali passed away quietly on June 3, 2016. In the days and weeks that followed, much was written and remembered about The Greatest. Tributes poured in from famous athletes, movie stars, humanitarians, politicians, and even American presidents, past and present. Muhammad Ali had touched so many people's lives in so many ways that it seemed the remembrances were never-ending.

But how best to remember Muhammad Ali? How did *Ali* want to be remembered? When asked several years earlier, Ali had expressed it simply and, of course, with a touch of humor:

"I would like to be remembered as a man who never looked down on those who looked up to him . . . who stood up for his beliefs . . . who tried to unite all humankind through faith and love. And if that's too much, then I guess I'd settle for being remembered only as a great boxer who became a leader and champion of his people.

"And I wouldn't even mind if folks forgot how pretty I was."